How are we to face the end of time— and the beginning of eternity?

Though this book is designed for group study, it is also intended for personal enjoyment and spiritual growth. A leader's guide is available from your local bookstore or your publisher.

Beacon Hill Press of Kansas City
Kansas City, Missouri

Editor
Everett Leadingham

Editorial Assistant
Carolyn Clements

Editorial Committee
Philip Baisley
Randy Cloud
David Felter
David Higle
Everett Leadingham
Thomas Mayse

Cover design by Kevin Williamson

Copyright 1996
by Beacon Hill Press of Kansas City
ISBN 083-411-5794
Printed in the United States of America

Bible Credits
Unless otherwise indicated, Scripture quotations in this book are taken from the *Holy Bible, New International Version*® (NIV®). Copyright © 1973, 1978, 1984 by International Bible Society. Used by permission of Zondervan Publishing House. All rights reserved.

The Scripture quotations that are marked KJV are taken from the King James Version.

10   9   8   7   6   5

CONTENTS

INTRODUCTION

Everything comes to an end. A good mystery novel has a final page. A career draws to a close at retirement. A person's life on earth ceases when death makes its claim. Someday the whole world as we know it will end.

Most of us are quite curious about those last two endings—our own death and the end of the world. They have such a strong hold on our curiosity because of the unanswered questions they pose. We wonder what death will be like and how the world will end because both events will have a serious impact on us.

Interest in the end of the world is growing almost daily. The secular media keeps the topic in the forefront with discussions about environmental concerns. Religious leaders continue to teach a wide variety of views on the subject.

In the midst of this widespread interest, most people find themselves confused or fearful—or both. In this book we do not want to contribute to further confusion or fear. We want to share the hope we Christians have in Jesus Christ.

Dialog Series books are meant to stimulate discussion. This one is no exception. Our purpose is to help small groups discuss the two most important endings—the personal death awaiting each of us and the second coming of Christ. Our goal is to enable participants to arrive at a clearly Wesleyan approach to "last things." The Wesleyan position inspires hope because it is firmly rooted in the grace of God.

Because these topics have the ability to produce confusion and fear, the discussions may be uncomfortable at times. And because many persons hold strong opinions about the subject of the Second Coming, discussing the subject in a gentle and loving manner may be difficult. It is our prayer that a spirit of openness, compassion, and humbleness will characterize every discussion in this book. We have tried to present all sides fairly and accurately.

Wesleyan scholars who have covered this territory before us have stated our purpose well. H. Orton Wiley, a prominent Holiness theologian of the previous generation, said this:

> At the outset, I may say that I have considerable hesitancy in discussing this. . . . A subject that has caused such a variety of opinion should be approached cautiously, and this we have sought to do. On subjects which are not clearly revealed, one should speak with becoming modesty. Those who speak with such a degree of positiveness as to exclude the sincere thought of Bible students who hold different positions are neither wise nor reverent. My design, therefore, is to present the material . . . suggestively, rather than dogmatically, and we trust that the statements here made will serve to provoke further study and research. . . . There is enough given us in the Scriptures to furnish the Church with a glorious hope; but the events can never be untangled until prophecy passes into history, and we view them as standing out clearly in their historical relations.[1]

More recent Holiness scholars have expressed our purpose in these words:

> While there is not likely to be unanimity of opinion concerning this complex issue, there may be mutual charity. Above all there must be unity of devotion to the Christ who came once according to promise, and assured us He would come again. Such devotion will prove itself in faithful service, constant readiness, and loving expectation.[2]

We offer this book to guide your discussions of important last things from a Wesleyan-Holiness perspective. And we echo what John wrote to conclude the Book of Revelation: "He who testifies to these things says, 'Yes, I am coming soon.' Amen. Come, Lord Jesus" (Revelation 22:20).

1. H. Orton Wiley, *Christian Theology*, 3 vols. (Kansas City: Beacon Hill Press, 1940-43), 3:306-7.
2. W. T. Purkiser, Richard S. Taylor, and Willard H. Taylor, *God, Man, and Salvation: A Biblical Theology* (Kansas City: Beacon Hill Press of Kansas City, 1977), 648.

SECTION I

Introductory Thoughts

by Richard Eckley

Richard Eckley, Ph.D., is assistant professor
of Christian ministries at Houghton College,
Houghton, New York.

IMPORTANT WORDS IN THIS CHAPTER

See *Glossary* for definitions.

Apocalypse

Apocalyptic

Covenant

Dispensation

Dispensationalism

Eschatology

Heresy

Heretical

Marxism

Messiah

Messianic

Millennium

Near-death experience

Omnipresence

Omniscience

Rationalist

Second Coming

Theism

Theistic

Tribulation

CHAPTER 1

Why Are "Last Things" Important?

MY FATHER RECALLS THE TINY CHURCH THAT I WAS raised in being full on the night of October 30, 1938. On that eve of Halloween, Orson Welles read a radio dramatization of H. G. Wells's *War of the Worlds*, a story about an invasion of earth by Martians. So realistic was the performance that, in spite of assurances it was only a play, millions of listeners panicked over visions of rampaging monsters and burning cities. With the end so near, people all over the country—and in that small mining town—wanted to get their lives in order.

We have a fascination with the end, whether our own demise or the end of the world. News reports daily bring us stories of tragic deaths. Most people have been acquainted with someone who has recently died. The reflection of an aging body reinforces the fact of our mortality every time we look into our mirror. Such realities raise questions in the human mind. *What happens when we die? Where do we go? When will I die? What will that be like?* Although most of the time we can ignore the questions about our personal death, it suddenly becomes important when we teeter on the brink of a crisis. As we ponder our personal end, we suddenly get serious about eternity.

The subject of the end of the world arises nearly everywhere we turn. We can hold a Sunday School class on the Book of Revelation, and people will flock to the course. Or we can read the morning paper or watch television and hear secular sources asking, "Can humanity survive another millennium?"

An Age-old Concern

People have always wondered about the end, because death is a part of the human condition. Ancient human beings had to deal with death at a much earlier age than modern humans. Perhaps much of the ancient civilizations' philosophy of life resulted from their trying to deal with the everyday reality of death. They introduced stories to explain their experience. Although the explanations varied by civilization, the common factor of all ancient cultures was coping with death by finding ways to survive human mortality.

The pyramids of Egypt stand as monuments to a human desire for immortality. Pointing to the heavens, they reflected that civilization's belief that their lives did not end with death. They mummified rulers and packed up tools in preparation for a long journey. They believed this life was over, but a new one had begun.

Ancient Chinese dynasties buried their leaders in long boats to make the trip into immortality, accompanied by terra-cotta soldiers to serve them in the next life. Other ancient civilizations erected stone posts on which they carved their history so the rest of the world would not forget that they had lived here.

Despite such wishes to survive death, real hope of surviving past death came only with the appearance of Jesus Christ into the world. A sense of a glorious end of history developed as Christians stood gazing into the clouds, waiting for their Savior to return.

We Are Not Always Right

One way of making sense of time is to chop it up into concise, thematic chunks. Christians have always understood God's work as coming in "dispensations"—most notably the periods of the old and new covenants. The millennium (a period of 1,000 years) is a biblical, and nicely rounded, number for a long dispensation of time. The desire to see King David's unified monarchy return to Israel was at its peak about 1,000 years (one millennium) after its collapse. This messianic expectation coincided with the birth of Jesus.

Yet, Christians throughout the centuries since Christ have not always thought correctly about the end. Montanus, in A.D. 150, prophesied that the second coming of Christ was about to happen. He even said that the plain of Phrygia was to be the place where the New Jerusalem would descend. Montanus was wrong. Nevertheless, this did not dispel many of his followers from meeting yearly on an adjacent mountaintop to wait for the end of the world.

Other Christians throughout the first 10 centuries also were expecting the world to end in their lifetimes. Tertullian of Carthage reported the descent of the New Jerusalem around Carthage in A.D. 200. Cyprian, also of Carthage, felt the end was near in 250. Adamnan of Iona (Scotland) was concerned about the end coming in 700.

Not surprisingly, the messianic expectations were still felt 1,000 years (one millennium) after Jesus had announced the Kingdom's arrival. Although scholars disagree about the extent of the anxiety, apprehension and fear marked the transition from the first to the second millennium. On New Year's Eve, A.D. 999, cattle and sheep were left to wander the mountainsides as crowds gathered in churches and pilgrims converged on the holy city of Jerusalem. "The end of the world being close, I hereby . . ." was the standard opening language of legal wills from that time. Certainly, that millennial year was distressful for individuals, even if the world was able to return to business as usual.

Despite the Church's warnings against such heretical views, theological charlatans still vex Christians today. Secular viewpoints highlight the fear of the planet's self-destruction by nuclear holocaust, ecological disaster, or worldwide famine and plague. Some religious leaders have played on this, asking their followers to sell all their earthly goods in exchange for community protection and isolation in the last days.

The world will not soon forget how David Koresh took his followers to a fiery death in a Waco, Texas, compound near the end of the second millennium A.D. Television viewers followed the tragic standoff with federal officials. Academic and religious experts explained the power this leader wielded to sway so many with his millennial views. One has to think that a proper understanding of the end could have saved these unfortunate lives.

Why Are We Interested in the End Times?

Why? For the first time since Noah, human beings can actually envision the end of all history. At many points in the history of the world, destruction came in a devastating form. Nevertheless, as bad as a plague seemed, it had only a local impact. Today is different. Today our communication is worldwide. Not only do we know about what happens at every place on the globe, but also the news affects us all. Many times that news has earthshaking implications. For example, a border skirmish in a remote area of the Middle East suddenly took on World War III dimensions as we watched in fascinated horror as the Gulf War unfolded in 1991.

We all, whether secular or religious, have reason to be interested in eschatology, or the study of last things.

The year A.D. 2000 is an arbitrary date on the Western calendar, but it is a significant marker for the contemporary generation. We grew up considering two common questions: "How old will I be?" and "What will I be doing in the year 2000?" The media also asked in a variety of ways, "What will life be like in the next millennium?" They constantly predicted new technology and human advancements.

A significant event occurred in the 20th century which made last things more interesting for Christians. In 1948 Israel became a country in the Middle East. In many minds this was a fulfillment of the words of Jesus: "Even so, when you see these things happening, you know that the kingdom of God is near. I tell you the truth, this generation will certainly not pass away until all these things have happened" (Luke 21:31-32). To think that we might be part of the final generation raised interest in the Second Coming.

Ill-informed radio and television hosts of Christendom have overshadowed the legitimate study of this important area of Christian concern. Often these teachers have increased anxiety over the approaching apocalypse rather than increasing faith.

The need to understand these compelling forces comes from the structures of our existence. They come as questions that we must answer if we are to go on living.

Questions about interpretation of historic events. The adjective "apocalyptic"—a name taken from a style of biblical literature found in the Books of Daniel, Revelation, and parts of the Gospels—describes the revealing of the hidden meanings behind our history. Events taking on apocalyptic proportions seem to happen almost daily in our times.

As with the scope of all recorded history, the modern day has had its share of puzzling features. The history of nations has surprised us with the miraculous reincarnation of Israel in 1948 and again with the collapse of the Soviet Union in the 1990s. The former begs to be understood in light of the promises made to Abraham. The latter has forced the hosts of the last-days talk shows to go back to the drawing board for a new "great Satan."

Questions relating to the world's survival. Ours is perhaps the first generation that can think the "unthinkable." Nuclear bombs have been a threat of worldwide destruction since 1945. Whether or not we built bomb shelters is not as important as how the fear became real as we looked at Hiroshima and political postures of superpowers.

Our increased knowledge of outer space has shown us the possibility that a stray comet could hit our planet and disintegrate us. Groups monitor the skies for such an event, prepared to intercept the errant comet with a destructive missile. This is not science fiction, but a known reality in our modern world.

Since Darwin, science has presented society with a picture of an evolving cosmos careening between a fragile balance and a chaotic collapse of nature. Ecologists develop theories to explain the consequences of cutting the rain forest down. They have warned us also that continuing to spew pollutants into the stratosphere will contribute to global warming and subsequent changing weather patterns. Pessimistic worldviews such as these point to the eventual terror—a time of tribulation over all the earth. We have come to understand our personal fate as tied to the fate of the cosmos.

Questions relating to human survival. Once humanity was much more optimistic about its own creative enterprise. Landing on the moon was the apex of human self-determination. John F. Kennedy's memorable speech announced the goal of a lunar landing, which was accomplished long after his own death. Through vaccines and medicine we cast aside the shackles of the human body. Yet, in spite of our medical genius, some germs have arisen that are resistant to our current medical technology. Any of them could encompass the globe and end life on this planet.

Now through genetic engineering we have initiated a reconstruction of the basic building blocks of creation. Technology has advanced so rapidly that our ethical thought and political institutions cannot keep up with the dilemmas created by it. Like Frankenstein, our tampering with life through science has created a monster threatening to turn on its master.

We have become acutely aware that most of life is outside our control. Diseases like cancer and AIDS have to date eluded our best attempts to conquer them. Massive atrocities, accompanied by television pictures of famine, earthquake, and flood victims, remind us that we live on the delicate line between life and extinction. We may not be far behind our extinct friends—the dinosaurs!

Sometimes even Christians feel overwhelmed by the seemingly evil forces. It is not hard to wonder if humans have a future.

Questions relating to God. The way in which we view the world has changed. For centuries, humans coped with the terrible events around them by trusting in God. No matter how bad the news, God was still in control. Today the typical worldview is much different. We seem to have worse news, and the question in many minds is, "Is God in charge?"

Instead of a reality believed by all, God's existence has become a question for many. Traditional theistic views, depicting God's personal involvement and control over history, are being challenged. Marxism is the best example of an atheistic alternative. Without God, humanity is the ruler and creator of its own destiny. Becoming increasingly popular among theologians is an evolutionary view of God in an attempt to understand the absurd realities of suffering in our world. This gives a view of God involved in the process of history—and constrained by it. This approach jettisons classic ideas of omniscience and omnipresence. The Creator is as surprised by the outcome of history as the creation is.

The fear of the future. Questions about what God can and cannot do about it. All this has created a greater need for understanding and hope, even among Christians.

Paul's correspondence to the Thessalonians was directed at the Early Church's first real questions. They were theological and practical: When was the second coming of Christ to occur? What was to become of those who did not live to see the end? Paul answered these difficulties with the assurance that, when the Lord returned, "the dead in Christ will rise first" (1 Thessalonians 4:16). Furthermore, they were to "encourage each other with these words" (v. 18). *The mark of any good eschatology is that it brings comfort and encouragement to our anxious questions.*

Where Do We Get Our Answers?

In an attempt to find the answers to these massive questions, people have turned to a variety of sources. It seems fear is a great market motivator.

Books. One or two books about near-death experiences are usually among the top 10 sellers on any secular booklist. Christian bookstores multiply books on the end times. Nearly every month two or three books about the end of the world are among the best-sellers.

Many evangelical Christians have received all their information on these subjects from popular writers like Hal Lindsey, C. I. Scofield, and John F. Walvoord. All these writers represent a type of rationalist exposé on the Book of Revelation. On the other hand, writers like Bruce Metzger, a New Testament scholar, offers his book, *Breaking the Code,* as a call for a "disciplined imagination" when dealing with these kinds of texts.

Adding to these Bible commentators, a new group of futurist writers, often emphasizing economic and global factors, has come on the horizon to "inform" our generation of impending doom. The history of Israel and the Middle East. Concern over the global economic market. The changing face of nationalism in the wake of the Soviet collapse toward a so-called one-world government. All these have fueled these conspiracy-laden interpretations. At one extreme the survivalists are selling us bunkers and machine guns, and at the other financiers cash in on our investments in gold bullion.

Hollywood. Science fiction has long heralded a time when humanity would rise from the ashes of its own future destruction. Star wars, a planet of apes, and mutants from nuclear disaster have given our culture new metaphors of hope.

Another variety—this one from the dark side—has captivated those interested in the demonic impulses of history. Theaters have record attendances for horror releases. Thanks to these films, "the Antichrist," "666," and "the seven seals" of the Apocalypse are biblical terms known very well by the general, moviegoing public. The audience goes away with a sense of the cosmic clash between good and evil. Nevertheless, evil is obviously the really big seller at the box office.

Prophets. Historically, prophets claiming to speak for a variety of gods attracted people struggling with the need to understand their role in history. Nostradamus, who lived from A.D. 1503 to 1566, predicted the future in a series of 100-year blocks in his work *The Centuries*. Nostradamus's predictions are vague and open to many interpretations. Consequently, people today still read current events into his predictions, which include a cataclysmic end of the world in 1999. Astrologers (perhaps Nostradamus's modern counterpart) offer people assurances for their personal questions. Some people find comfort in the face of life's uncertainty by believing that the consistent harmony of the stars and planets direct their lives.

Cults. Cults have often preyed upon people's fears by presenting a systemic and cohesive end-times philosophy. Traditional cults, such as Jehovah's Witnesses and Mormons, give their adherents a very sophisticated understanding of what will happen at the end of history, even down to the details of their marriages and homes. New Age, an Eastern-like religion, has added a slant with no idea of history, assuring the individual that he or she can be released from the constraints of history and meld into the universe. This results in a positive psychological experience but gives little meaning to the struggles of this life.

The Bible. Christians turn to the Bible in the search for meaning about death and the end of the world. Although a variety of opinions arise among Christians, we know that God holds the answers to our deepest questions.

Christ came to earth as a human to show us what God is like. His resurrection instills true hope in us that physical death is not final destruction. The Bible is where Christians read about Jesus Christ's exemplary life, sacrificial death, and hope-inspiring resurrection.

Christians ultimately believe that the answers to our end-of-the-world questions are found in the Bible as well. Christians, as anyone else, are concerned about the end. However, the Church has learned through Jesus Christ to rely upon God's timetable rather than human schemes. A thoughtful look at the subjects of death and the end of the world should bring a sense of hope and comfort to the believer.

Background Scripture: Luke 21:31-32; 1 Thessalonians 4:16, 18

IMPORTANT WORDS IN THIS CHAPTER

See *Glossary* for definitions.

Cyclical time

Linear time

Immanence

Transcendence

Wesleyan

CHAPTER 2

What Time Is It?

"AND THAT'S THE WAY IT IS, TUESDAY, NOVEMBER 12
. . ." Walter Cronkite ended each day's newscast with his familiar refrain and the date. He reminded the listener that the events of the world had been recorded and that we were moving on. The calendar day was a folder of events placed in the great file cabinet of time.

Libraries, archives, and the science of history itself catalog the events of our past. Most existing cultures have come to believe in the need to know their past. Even ancient civilizations told stories about heroic gods and legendary leaders that gave meaning to their contemporary situation. These epics, while not necessarily history by modern standards, did give significance to their place in time.

What Time Is It?

Certainly at a personal level we are aware that time is relative. While waiting to find out the results of a test to discover a disease threatening the life of their child, a couple sitting in the waiting room may find that time "drags on." This same couple, aboard a vacation cruise, might find that five days of fun and relaxation just "fly by."

The elusive quality of time has led to our new interest in time management. We can speak of "time well spent," or we can "waste time." Through an array of appointment books and computer programs, the wise can use every waking minute to its fullest potential. Time does not have to control us; we can manage it.

More important than organizing time so that it can be controlled is the need to order it to bring a sense of meaning to our lives. Prisoners of war and of society, hostages, and astronauts all have testified to the inbred need while in isolation to order their time. Sometimes this has been done by the sun and the moon, sometimes by the human body's own internal clock. Psychologically, we need to understand our lives in an ordered and meaningful way.

Even though we use the English word "time" in a variety of meanings, the Greek language has separate words for distinct aspects of time. This makes the usage more clear.

A Greek word, *chronos*, describes the measure of time, like seconds, minutes, and hours. We use the *chronos* aspect of time to get to work and church "on time." When someone asks, "What time is it?" they are looking for an answer in chronological time. We are also speaking of *chronos* when we catalog the events of days, weeks, and years.

However, when we attach meaning to those events, we are using a different aspect of time. Another Greek term, *kairos*, emphasizes meaningfulness of time. This is the concept we use when we remember the significance of an event more than the date it occurred.

If we look at two examples from Jesus' own words, the distinction in usage will be clear. In John 7:33, He says to His disciples, "I am with you for only a short time *[chronos]*, and then I go to the one who sent me."

But in verse 8, He tells them, "You go to the Feast. I am not yet going up to this Feast, because for me the right time *[kairos]* has not yet come." In the first instance Jesus is talking about the few, short years He has spent with the disciples. In the second case He is referring to the meaningful time that was yet to come—the events of His crucifixion and resurrection.

Models of Time

Like individual people, cultures have tended to order time in ways that are meaningful to their existence. We can distinguish two basic ways to view time.

Cyclical. In the ancient world, many of Israel's neighbors saw time as cyclical. They watched as plants sprang up from the ground, gave forth their fruit, and died. Birth and death completed the cycle of life. The preacher of Ecclesiastes said it this way: "There is a time for everything, and a season for every activity under heaven: a time to be born and a time to die, a time to plant and a time to uproot" (3:1-2).

It's not surprising that agricultural societies tended to order their calendars along this line. Harvest and thanksgiving celebrations, fertility cults and sacrifices, all intermingled in a remembrance of past bounty and future needs. Growing seasons followed dormant periods in the fields. Such yearly cycles became a model by which the community could reflect on the questions of human life and death.

The underlying belief of a cyclical view is that time is repetitive. Because it is repetitive, the future will be recognizable and predictable. The future will look a lot like the past.

I worked in a nursing home for several years while in college. John* lived all his life in that institution. He once told me every day was the same there. People all around him wore white uniforms; his dinner came like clockwork; and even the holidays were rhythmic interruptions on the nursing station calendar. When it came time for me to graduate, I went to tell John good-bye. Taking a long drag on his cigarette, he merely said, "There were people who worked here before you. I'm sure someone will come to take your place." He turned his face toward the window and exhaled his smoke.

Seeing time as an unending cycle can lead to a pessimistic view. It is easy for such persons to feel, or even say, "We're stuck. There's nothing we can do. Everything just goes around over and over." For them life's cycle is inescapable and unchangeable.

*Name has been changed.

Yet other persons view an unending cycle of time in a positive way. The unchangeableness gives them a feeling of security. Since the cycle is always the same, life is predictable and stable.

In a cyclical view, time never ends. Time continues as an endless series of cycles. However, events are never repeated exactly. Repetitions occur, but always there is a sense of forward progress. Each new cycle teaches things that can improve the next go-round. Things can get better with each repetition.

The concept of progress—the idea that time is moving in a cumulative and positive direction—is still a strong belief in the world. However, with the arrival of modern atheism and its rejection of the Judeo-Christian view that time ends in God, this view has brought great anxiety to many. The world continues to believe that time is leading somewhere, but without a belief in God they have no idea where.

Few would deny that we can see cycles in life and discern similarities between the present event and some past event. We can see the impact individual persons have. We all like to think that we contribute something during our time, and that the future is better for what we have done. There is a sense of anticipation that the next cycle of events will bring new and exciting possibilities.

Linear. However, Christianity does not view history as an unending cycle of events leading to a general sense of progress. A linear view holds that time moves forward in a line toward a finite end. Christians believe that God created time and has intentionally engaged in relationship with humans within the framework of time. They also believe He will bring time to an end somewhere in the future.

From the time that God told Abram to go to a place that He would show him, the Hebrews understood their future to be somewhere in front of them. The Lord God Almighty was not tied to any locality, as other ancient Near Eastern gods were, but led Israel through life as a pillar of fire and smoke. The idea of hope was born in the suffering of God's people in their various captivities and tied to the future Promised Land of rest.

Christians have a unique way of looking at occurrences in time. The biblical view sees these events as "salvation history." Two aspects of this are important. First, salvation's story unfolds along a continuous time line. The line had a unique beginning point and moves in a direct fashion toward an end. Second, all events along this straight line are related to the important event at the midpoint—the death and resurrection of Jesus.

The Christ-event introduces eternity into the human time line. While we live our lives bound by the limitations of being human, we can see in Jesus a glimpse of the eternal salvation God has brought into our world. We could say that the event of Jesus, in the middle of the story, was the end of the story brought backward in time. While we live in the middle, we can also see the end of time. The writer of Hebrews described it like this: "Yet at present we do not see everything subject to him. But we see Jesus" (2:8-9). Paul understood this to affect our perceptions when he wrote, "Now I know in part; then I shall know fully" (1 Corinthians 13:12). The unforgettable phrase in the Gloria Patri, "World without end," is a reminder that eternity has been brought into time through Jesus Christ.

In contrast to a despairing cyclical view of time, the Christian view is marked with hope. The role of the Holy Spirit in our lives is to be a guarantee of what we are to receive at the end of time—redemption. Therefore, we have difficulty identifying with people who see life as hopeless.

An illustration of this can be seen in the struggle of two college roommates. They would come home from class each day to a rat-infested apartment and eat cold beans from a can. They would fill their days with humor and dreams to remind themselves that this life would not continue. Yet for many of their friends such a life was unending. The rats, the squalor, and the dread would be there tomorrow—and into the days after. The roommates knew that they could endure such conditions in order to graduate and move on to better days. For them, education was the difference between hope and despair. Christians, mindful of the hope Christ has promised, can endure present conditions by looking forward to the end.

We are all people who live in the in-between time. Our past is behind us in a gray cloud. The farther we look back, the less we can see. Our future also looms before us as an unknown. Jesus Christ came into the middle of the story to show us its end. (John shows that this event also reveals the beginning of time as well.) Ever since that historic event, we have dated our calendars B.C., "before Christ," and A.D., "in the year of our Lord" [from the Latin words *anno Domini*].

God in Time and Eternity

Time is a deep subject for humans to contemplate. We are bound within the finite; that is, there are definite limits to what we can comprehend. God, however, is infinite. He understands everything perfectly. Our inability to think of time as He does in no way limits His actions.

Because we are limited in understanding God's eternal perspective, we arrange our story so we can understand life. Events by themselves appear chaotic. Because humans do not easily comprehend the multitude and variety of daily occurrences, we try to find meaningful patterns in them. The day's events are a mere collection of names, places, and happenings, often coming to us in a blur. Questions like "What is going on?" or "Why did this happen?" arise from these experiences. For Christians the important question is, more deeply, "What is God doing in the world?"

Christians believe that God has invaded time, and we often talk about the story of salvation in this way. The Apostles' Creed, long recited by the Church as a touchstone of faith, says: "I believe . . . in Jesus Christ . . . born of the Virgin Mary, suffered under Pontius Pilate . . ." We are reminded that the coming of Jesus was a historical event associated with real people and places.

However, a more significant meaning for our discussion of the Christian understanding of time is the aspect of meaningfulness. For example, the preacher in Ecclesiastes reminds us: "[God] has made everything beautiful in its time. He has also set eternity in the hearts of men; yet they cannot fathom what God has done from beginning to end" (3:11). Galatians 4:4 says: "But when the time had fully come, God sent his Son." The revelation of God in the person of Jesus Christ has given meaning to all of human time.

Theologians have speculated just how this intersection of God and human time works. They perceive God's role in the story along a continuum of transcendence and immanence. Some believers in transcendence would paint a picture of a God so distant that the world is literally on its own. At the other end of the spectrum, those who stress immanence would have such an involved God that the story is dissolved into no distinction between human and divine. As with the most difficult questions, the truth is found somewhere in the middle.

Radical transcendence. Some persons think that because God either does not exist or is incapable of interfering with His creation, humankind must direct its own state of affairs. They view the human story as self-fulfilled and determined. Atheism, deism, and agnosticism could be described as models of radical transcendence.

We have written most of modern history from this point of view. The trajectories of human events are seen driven by the impulses of greed, ingenuity, or even chance. To the scientific mind, God is irrelevant to the sequence of cause and effect in human deeds.

Radical immanence. In this view God's participation in human events is so close that God himself is affected—and often left powerless. Models such as pantheism (God is equal to the created order) and process theology (God is a partner in our suffering) emphasize such close participation of God in the story.

Since World War II, a pessimistic understanding of God's role in time has dominated Western faith. Holocaust historian Elie Wiesel relates the gruesome story of a small boy on a Nazi gallows. Fellow prisoners were required to watch as the boy hung between heaven and earth, too light to die quickly. Overheard from the Jewish spectators were the words, "Where is God now?" Wiesel inwardly responded: "Here He is—hanging on the gallows."

This grotesque picture makes us feel better about a God who is personally and compassionately involved in human events. God experiences the painful twists of the story just as we do. At the same time, it presents us with an anemic God quite powerless to intervene and stop the catastrophic events of time—or even our personal lives. Ultimately this despair led theologians of the 1960s to declare the "death" of God.

A middle ground. Christians have historically supported the idea that a personal God is involved with the creation. At the same time, the Creator is still distinct from it. We derive an understanding of salvation history from this view. We believe that within the events of time, God is directing and cooperating with humanity to save the world.

Why would we pray if we did not believe that the God to whom we pray also acts? Hope and belief are born in the Christian's experience that God listens and seeks to direct our lives and the fate of the world.

The discussion of chronological time and meaningful time can lead one to ask the questions: "Can we really know what time it is?" or "Do we even care?" Christians answer in the affirmative. We do know what time it is. Because of Jesus Christ, we are already living in the end times. We know the end of the story now. Furthermore, we care about the nature of the story. We derive personal and public meaning from a proper interpretation of time. Christians live every day knowing that the Alpha and Omega—the Beginning and the End—is in control.

Background Scripture: Ecclesiastes 3:1-2, 11; John 7:8, 33; 1 Corinthians 13:12; Galatians 4:4; Hebrews 2:8-9

SECTION II

The End of
Personal Life

by Carl Leth

Carl Leth, Ph.D., is senior pastor of the
North Raleigh Church of the Nazarene,
Raleigh, North Carolina.

Important Word in This Chapter

See *Glossary* for definition.

Reincarnation

CHAPTER 3

Death Stalks Us All

IT WAS MARIE WHO REALLY INTRODUCED ME TO death. I knew about death, of course. I had known people who died. I had attended—and even officiated at—funerals. Still, somehow death had been kept at arm's length—a safe, impersonal distance. Marie changed that for me. She was a friend of a person in my church. She was dying of cancer, and she was not a Christian. That is, not until our second visit. There in her hospital room as I read a psalm, her tears flowed and her heart opened. From that moment I knew that she and I would walk this last journey together. Over the next few months I watched her body waste away and her soul come alive. In a special relationship that only God could explain, I became her companion for this journey through death's valley. It was in walking with Marie through that valley that I really came to know death. I learned to see death's ugliness, to experience God's gracious hope, and to lose my fear of this terrible enemy.

Facing the reality of death is something we try to avoid. We live in a death-denying culture. Age and death are so disturbing to us that we have become a youth-worshiping culture. Any product that can keep us young, or even help us maintain the illusion of youth, is sure to draw a market. We often avoid the elderly. Increasingly isolated in "homes" for the elderly, they no longer intrude into our daily lives with their reminder of life's swift passing.

Our reluctance to face the reality of death prevents us from preparing for death. People put off making wills. Important business or family decisions are left unmade. Most avoid the sensible and financially prudent opportunity for "pre-need" funeral planning. Even in the face of serious illness, we often avoid discussion of the prospect of coming death.

Other societies and cultures have been more realistic, even matter-of-fact, about the prospect of death. In the late Middle Ages, a handbook on the art of dying was a best-seller, published in multiple editions. Death was an inescapable reality to be faced realistically and practically. Death was a part of the common experience of human life. So it remains in many countries and cultures around the world today. Especially in areas of the world where death is a more frequent companion, it is faced more openly.

Somehow in our culture we have attempted to remove the reality of death from common experience. The dead are swiftly whisked away by professional strangers. They reappear only briefly, if at all, in as lifelike a state as possible. Our public grief is muted. We studiously avoid reference to death itself. The deceased has "passed away," "departed," or "gone on." We can hardly bring ourselves to say the words "died," "dead," or "death."

When Joseph Bayly wrote his book on death for our culture, he titled it *The Last Thing We Talk About*. Nevertheless, the reality remains that, whether we talk about it or not, death is a part of human existence. It is an unavoidable prospect looming darkly in each of our futures. Death surrounds us. Television brings its graphic reality into our homes daily. Our local newspapers tell sad and tragic tales of young and old victims of unexpected death. We encounter funeral processions on the streets. Even in the church we are constantly reminded of death as we are asked to pray for those families whom it has touched.

Some who are reading this are uncomfortable already, wishing we could talk about something else. Sadly, our fear of death and our avoidance and denial of its reality simply make death a more difficult topic to discuss. Happily for us as Christians, this is not necessary. We can face the reality and challenge of death honestly and in hope.

Understanding Death

Death is an abnormality. We did not need to experience death. When God created Adam and Eve in the garden, death was not part of the plan. God created humankind to enjoy fellowship with Him forever. This does not mean that He created us as immortal souls independent of himself. That idea comes from ancient Greek philosophy rather than Scripture. Still, God created us for eternal life with himself. Death is the result of Satan's intrusion into God's plan for life.

Life is a gift of God. "For in him we live and move and have our being" (Acts 17:28). It is in relationship with God that we know life. We do not have life independent of God. To be separated from God is to be separated from life, to die. Sin condemned humankind to an existence of slow death. The death of our natural bodies is the result of sin's impact on our earthly existence. "Sin entered the world through one man, and death through sin, and in this way death came to all men, because all sinned" (Romans 5:12). Death is a consequence of sin.

We have all become the inheritors of sin's penalty. Even innocent, little children are subject to it. The terrifying incidence of crib death is a striking reminder that death is a relentless foe in human existence. Sinful, destructive behaviors may hasten physical death, but personal purity is not a protection from it.

Death is the ultimate expression of sin's aggression against God. It is Satan's attempt to destroy life as God created it. It is the claim of the enemy, displayed in the flesh, that the power of sin and death has mastered the power of life.

Overcoming Death

It should produce no surprise that dealing with the fearsome prospect of death prompts our attention and energy.

Apart from the hope of Christ, our culture has very little it can bring to the problem. Attempts to resist or avoid death are a persistent feature of human society. The multifaceted search for the Fountain of Youth attempts to find a way to escape—even temporarily—the inevitability of death. Nevertheless, they all meet with meager success. This forces our society's retreat into denial. We attempt to ignore death, to act as if it is not real. We pretend that death will not come to us. That is why we so often meet death with surprise.

Our cultural denial of death attempts to ignore the power of death. We cannot face the prospect that death brings the *end* for us. We ease our fears about the limits of our mortality by persuading ourselves of our immortality. Reincarnation is a currently popular way to avoid death's reality and life-ending power. Popular conceptions of some vague, but pleasant, immortality help ease our distress. We try to convince ourselves that death's power is an illusion.

Like generations before us, we work to create monuments that will leave our mark on the world and so overcome death. We comfort ourselves that we will, in some way, continue to "be." We leave monuments of stone, wealth, art, or power. They are, however, only false, or at best limited, sources of comfort. The centers of our cities hold decaying buildings and homes that were exhibitions of status and power. The memory of most of those who built them has not lasted as long as the buildings. Family and hangers-on contest fortunes amassed over a lifetime, often in frivolous waste. The names and lives of artists who were leading figures in their time are now often forgotten by all except historians.

No matter what monument we leave behind to memorialize our lives, ultimately we arrive at the place of Shelley's "Ozymandias."

> *I met a traveller from an antique land*
> *Who said: "Two vast and trunkless legs of stone*
> *Stand in the desert . . ."*
> . . . .
> *"My name is Ozymandias, king of kings:*
> *Look on my works, ye Mighty, and despair!"*

Nothing beside remains. Round the decay
Of that colossal wreck, boundless and bare
The lone and level sands stretch far away.[1]

The world's helplessness in the face of death forces our society to practice systematic dishonesty by denying the reality and power of death. It has no other choice.

We Christians, however, can face death honestly, realistically, and with hope. For us, death's victory is a hollow and temporary one. First Corinthians 15:50-58 offers a rousing victory shout of the Christian's triumph over death. We need not pretend that death is somehow a friend or a pleasant prospect in our future. Death is an ugly thing. It is Satan's desperate attempt to extinguish the life that God has created. Nevertheless, death is a temporary victor, a hollow conqueror, for those whose life is in Christ.

Facing Death

Our Christian faith enables us to face honestly the reality, power, and ugliness of death and, yet, to face death with assurance and hope. We celebrate and enjoy life as a gift of God and an expression of His gracious goodness. We understand death as an ugly enemy of the life God has created. We can face death in confident hope because we know that what Satan intends for evil God has turned to good. Satan gleefully observed the death of Jesus Christ on the Cross. Then he woefully witnessed His resurrection from the grave.

In Christ's resurrection, He overcame death itself for us. "For as in Adam all die, so in Christ all will be made alive" (1 Corinthians 15:22). Death's temporary victory was followed by death's ultimate defeat. This truth gives us courage to face death. A repentant William Laud, facing execution as an old man, expressed the powerful encouragement we may find in Christ's victory over death. He prayed, "I am coming, oh, Lord! as quickly as I can. I know I must pass through death before I come to Thee, but it is only a mere shadow—a little darkness upon nature: Thou hast broken the jaws of death."[2]

As Christians, we have a sure hope in Jesus Christ. Yet this does not mean that we are indifferent to the prospect of death. How should we expect, as Christians, to face death? Is it natural to have some anxiety about death? Yes, even for Christians death is a bitter enemy. It represents the unknown, at least about the process of death. We may be sure of our final destination, but none of us knows what the journey through death is like.

Is it wrong to feel grief and sorrow at the prospect of death? No, for Scripture records that even Jesus experienced those feelings. Feeling sadness at separation from those we love is natural. Is it necessary to live in fear of death? No, for Christ is greater than death. Christ empowers us to face life's final enemy in confident hope. When we can say with Paul, "I have fought the good fight, I have finished the race, I have kept the faith," we may also say with a sure and confident hope, "Now there is in store for me the crown of righteousness, which the Lord, the righteous Judge, will award to me on that day." We might add with Paul, "And not only to me, but also to all who have longed for his appearing" (2 Timothy 4:7-8).

That's where my journey with Marie was interrupted. We finally reached the point where she had to go on without me. Death claimed her for its own, but she and I knew better. Death could claim her, but it could not keep her. We had seen death's ugly face and felt its destructive power. We had also discovered its ultimate defeat.

"'Where, O death, is your victory?

Where, O death, is your sting?'

. . . thanks be to God! He gives us the victory through our Lord Jesus Christ" (1 Corinthians 15:55, 57).

1. Percy Bysshe Shelley, "Ozymandias," 1817.
2. Herbert Lockyer, *Last Words of Saints and Sinners* (Grand Rapids: Kregel, 1969), 156-57.

Background Scripture: Acts 17:28; Romans 5:12; 1 Corinthians 15:22, 50-58; 2 Timothy 4:7-8

IMPORTANT WORDS IN THIS CHAPTER

See *Glossary* for definitions.

Buddhism

Hinduism

Near-death experience

Reincarnation

Resurrection

Chapter 4

What's Beyond Death?

To sleep: Perchance to dream: ay, there's the rub:
For in that sleep of death what dreams may come,
When we have shuffled off this mortal coil,
Must give us pause.[1]

SHAKESPEARE'S SOMBER HAMLET EXPRESSES A COMmon concern. What happens after death? That question casts its long shadow over much of life. How we answer that question shapes not only our approach to death but also our approach to life. Is there something more? Is this all there is? Our difficulty in answering the question is only increased by our lack of direct evidence or personal knowledge. The afterlife is beyond the reach of our experience. The practice of communicating with the dead or the search for memories of some prior existence are attempts to peek beyond death's curtain. We have not, however, found them persuasive or reassuring. Recent interest in near-death experiences has also expressed our desire to know what is beyond. But even these experiences leave us with many unanswered questions. We long for some assurance. Yet we remain in the uncomfortable position of facing the inevitable and unknowable prospect of what waits beyond death.

Cultural Understanding of the Afterlife

The sense that there is something after death is, in fact, a persistent characteristic of human society. Throughout history and in virtually every culture there has been some belief in an existence after death. The great pyramids of the ancient Egyptians are monuments to their faith, or at least hope, in an afterlife. They stocked royal tombs with provisions, servants, even transportation for use in the afterworld. The Egyptians mastered the process of mummification, which could preserve the body indefinitely. This process, which is a precursor to the modern practice of embalming, prepared the body for the afterlife. The burial process included everything that one would need for use in the world beyond this life.

Such beliefs in life after death are widespread among cultures. Modern excavations have uncovered an ancient Chinese burial site that included an army to accompany a deceased ruler into the afterlife. The Greeks—both in their philosophy and mythology—expressed a strong belief in continued existence after physical death. The Teutonic tribes of northern Europe, Norsemen of ancient Scandinavia, Incas, Mayans, and Aztecs of Central and South America all displayed a strong belief in the reality of an afterlife. Though expressed or understood in different ways, the expectation of some form of an afterlife has been historically affirmed by humankind. This broad, historical witness indicates the strength of the human conviction that there is something beyond death. It also portrays the uncertainty of the human understanding of what the afterlife holds. Humans seem sure that there is something after death, but they don't know what it is.

Buddhism and Hinduism understand the afterlife in terms of reincarnation. In varying forms this belief suggests that there is an eternal spiritual reality that recurs in a succession of physical lives. The individual personality is not reborn, but a spiritual connection continues in some way beyond death and into the next life. Ultimately, that identity is incorporated into a universal "self."

In the West, reincarnation is interpreted in more personal and individualistic terms. Contemporary New Age philosophies propose the continuing reincarnation of the same person, or conscious self. In this way persons may continue to exist as discrete personalities in successive lives. They pass on character traits, accumulated experience, and memories. Some teach that these memories, though clouded, may be rediscovered through flashes of recollection or by regressive hypnosis or therapy.

Near-death experiences are another currently popular "window" into life after death. Popular books, articles, and talk shows explore the near-death experience in its comforting aspect. Witnesses tell of warm light welcoming them into an experience of extraordinary peace. Commentators draw attention to the absence of any Christian faith or spiritual commitment in many of these witnesses. The implication of the omission is that Christian faith does not matter.

However, research by a practicing cardiologist into near-death experiences gives a different and more balanced report. He concludes that roughly 50 percent of near-death experiences are frightening and terror-filled.[2] Ultimately, of course, such experiences—good or bad—are not sufficient evidence to explain the afterlife. They are subjective and therefore are an inadequate foundation for knowing. Secular culture finally lacks the sure knowledge it seeks.

Christian Understanding of the Afterlife

Our Christian faith offers an answer to that dilemma. The Christian understanding of life after death is clear, consistent, and meaningful. It offers an understanding of death and life that makes sense and gives meaning to our existence. The claim that Christianity offers irrational or escapist explanations of life should be firmly rejected. In fact, the Christian faith offers a consistent and reasonable interpretation of our existence—including the questions of death and afterlife. We cannot scientifically prove the truth of our beliefs. We can, however, offer an explanation that empowers us to live in this life while giving us hope to face what comes after death.

The biblical record is occasionally ambiguous about the details of the afterlife but inescapably clear about the core of our understanding. "For God so loved the world that he gave his one and only Son, that whoever believes in him shall not perish but have eternal life" (John 3:16). God has made provision for us in Christ. He has given us an answer to the pressing questions of life and death. The Christian faith understands that we will, in fact, experience physical death in this life (unless we are still living when Jesus returns). We also understand that when He returns, those disciples who are dead will be resurrected and given a new and incorruptible body. (See 1 Corinthians 15:50-53.) It is important to note that the Christian understanding of life after death is a bodily, not merely spiritual, life. We are created as a combination of body and spirit, and we will exist in eternity as a combination of body and spirit.

The Bible does not give us a systematic description, but it does give us some provocative insights into the life that awaits Jesus' disciples. It includes the idea of transformation. We will be changed in dramatic and wonderful ways (1 Corinthians 15:50-55; 1 John 3:2). We will find ourselves in the immediate presence of God with all the blessing that implies (1 Thessalonians 4:17; John 14:2-3; Revelation 21:3-4). That life will include perfection in knowledge (1 Corinthians 13:9-12; 1 John 3:2). Finally, that life will be a state of blessedness, a wonderfully enhanced existence (Revelation 21:1-4; 22:1-5). Sustained by the Giver of life, we will enjoy an eternity in His presence. There we will be beyond the reach of sorrow, suffering, and pain (7:14-17; 21:3-4). We will enter a state of eternal glory (Romans 8:18; 2 Corinthians 4:17).

We are less clear about some details. For instance, what happens between our physical death and the resurrection? This theoretical question gains personal importance when death parts us from a loved one. How do we answer the child's tearful query, "Where is Grandma now?" Some have held that we enter a soul sleep until awakened by the last trumpet. Others hold that we go immediately into Christ's presence, returning in some way to participate in the Second Coming and final resurrection of the dead. Finding biblical evidence that seems to imply both options is possible. (For example: 1 Corinthians 15:50-55 and Luke 23:39-43.) Earnest and sincere Christians have held both views. Nevertheless, the strongest evidence supports the view that, at our death, we are translated into God's presence. There we retain conscious identity and experience a state of blessedness. This is an intermediate state, awaiting our final resurrection in a new body. Although some details are unclear, we can be confident that our next experience after death will be an awakening into the presence of God and the beginning of eternity with Him.

Facing the Unknown

Shakespeare's Hamlet poses the problem well. Death is that "undiscovered country from whose bourn* no traveler returns." The uncertainty of what happens after death is finally not possible to resolve this side of death. It is this uncertainty that prompts both our cultural attempts to dismiss the problem and our frantic attempts to solve it. Our culture struggles to find some basis of reassurance in this life that will help us face the life to come.

Skepticism may be a popular attitude in our society, but it makes a poor companion alongside our deathbed. Popular or primitive notions of some vaguely defined afterlife provide a weak foundation for faith when facing the certainty of death's power. Edward Gibbon, author of the great history *The Decline and Fall of the Roman Empire*, faced the poverty of his lack of faith in his hour of death. "This day may be my last. I will agree that the immortality of the soul is at times a very comfortable doctrine. All this is now lost, finally, irrevocably lost. All is dark and doubtful."[3]

In the fearsome face of death and the uncertainty of what follows, our society is left largely powerless to help us.

*An old word meaning boundary or destination.

Christianity offers us a positive alternative. As Christians, our faith guides and empowers us for life; but it also encourages us in the face of death. The Christian funeral is a time of celebration. This is not to disregard the real elements of sadness and loss even in a Christian death. Rather, amid the feelings of sorrow there is the recognition of a life safely entrusted to Christ. It can be the celebration of a life well lived and well invested.

We can't prove what we believe, but we can claim a consistent and meaningful explanation of life after death. We can offer a resolution of hope and meaning in the face of death. We may not be able to prove it, but we confidently believe that across the river of death stands One who waits to receive us. In fact, this confidence in the face of death is based upon our personal experience in *this* life.

We don't have personal knowledge of what waits beyond death, but we personally know and experience the One who waits for us beyond the shadow of death. He is the One who told His name to Moses when He called His people out of Egypt—"I AM WHO I AM" (Exodus 3:14). He declared, "This is my name forever, the name by which I am to be remembered from generation to generation" (v. 15). God was telling Moses He would always be with us. Those of us who are Christ's disciples can verify by personal experience that it is true. Repeatedly through life God has been faithful to us. Continually He has been present with us. We cannot directly know the life that awaits us after death, but we do know the One who will meet us there. Because He has been a familiar and faithful Companion in life, we can confidently expect Him to remain so in death. Based on our own experience in this life, we can draw assurance as we face the prospect of the life to come. We may not know the details of life after death, but we know Him.

Going Home

I recently heard it again. It seems to occur so often. A Christian was dying. Life was slipping away. Then something happened. She seemed to see something as she looked up at the ceiling above her bed. No, not some*thing*, but Some*one*. She seemed to speak to the One she saw. An expression of absolute peace came over her face. All tension and anxiety left her. She seemed even to smile with happiness. Then she was gone. Death had claimed her.

Yet not death alone. One had come to meet her, to take her hand as she passed under the shadow of death. Death's grim shadow is not dark enough to keep the light of hope from the dying Christian. For Jesus' disciple, "To live is Christ and to die is gain" (Philippians 1:21). Our lives are lived out of our faith in our resurrected and living Savior. We face our own death in the same faith.

Hamlet didn't quite get it right after all. One has traveled into the undiscovered country of death and returned. Beyond our uncertain step into death He waits for us. The words John Wesley called out at his death express the truth that may comfort and encourage us as we face the uncertainty of this dark passage: "The best of all, God is with us."[4]

1. William Shakespeare, *Hamlet*, act 3, scene 1.

2. Arline Brecher, "As Many Go to Hell as Heaven," in *Endtime: The Doomsday Catalog* (New York: Macmillan, 1979), 221.

3. Herbert Lockyer, *Last Words of Saints and Sinners* (Grand Rapids: Kregel, 1969), 131.

4. Arnold Lunn, *John Wesley* (New York: Dial Press, 1929), 355.

Background Scripture: Exodus 3:14-15; Luke 23:39-43; John 3:16; 14:2-3; Romams 8:18; 1 Corinthians 13:9-12; 15:50-55; 2 Corinthians 4:17; Philippians 1:21; 1 Thessalonians 4:17; 1 John 3:2; Revelation 7:14-17; 21:1-4; 22:1-5

Important Words in This Chapter

See *Glossary* for definitions.

Existentialism

Gehenna

Hades

Marxism

Materialism

Near-death experience

Nihilism

Rationalist

Reincarnation

Sheol

CHAPTER 5

Last Stop: Hell or Heaven?

WHAT IF THERE WERE NO HEAVEN OR NO HELL? What if there were no consequences beyond this life, no punishments and no rewards? Would it make life easier somehow? Are heaven and hell relics of religious belief that have no place in the modern world? Are they concepts that demean God and us? Or, could it be that they express something profound and meaningful that goes beyond the world's crude characterizations of them?

Some believe that without the prospect of reward or punishment, humanity would be able to usher in an era of peace and harmony. With the burdensome belief in an afterlife abandoned, they think we would find ourselves in an ideal unity. Such ideas strike a responsive chord with a large segment of our generation. Rejection of a belief in heaven and hell is a popular notion.

Yet our culture bombards us with conflicting popularized notions of reincarnation, communication with the dead, and near-death experiences that "affirm" an afterlife—all expressions of a belief or desire to reach beyond death. Most people seem to share a common interest in the afterlife, but we have mixed ideas about what comes after death.

Any belief in the afterlife must answer the question, "What happens after death?" What is the nature of that future existence? Is it an unconditional transition into some blissful state? Is it a shadow world of unhappiness and diminished personal identity? Is it an experience of torment and punishment?

Ancient Greek mythology proposed a dark underworld, populated by the dead, surrounded by the dark river Styx. They called it Hades after the Greek god who ruled it. Upon arrival, the dead were judged and committed, either to everlasting torment or to the blessedness of the Elysian Fields.[1]

Dante's *Divine Comedy* graphically describes the levels of hell and the torments of its occupants. Renaissance artists portrayed the horrors of hell in scenes every bit as terrifying as any modern horror film. Modern writers have speculated on more psychological states of torment, as in Sartre's *No Exit*. They remind us that unending life can easily become a state of torment through the human limitations and faults we bring to it.

Contemporary culture generally selectively adapts the traditional Christian concept of heaven and hell. We reject the unpleasant notion of existence in hell and promote an alternative idea of the blessedness of a heavenly afterlife. We choose the comforting expectation of an enjoyable, even enhanced, existence after death while dismissing the ideas of judgment or punishment as cruel and outdated. We might keep the threat of hell for the truly evil but not for the rest of us. A blessed reward is sure to follow even a minimally moral life. It is somehow satisfying to think that those who have earned our personal judgment will receive appropriate punishment. It is uncomfortably disturbing to consider that possibility for ourselves.

Primarily, modern humans have practiced skepticism about an afterlife and judgment. The materialism of Marxism, the despair of existentialism, and the extreme pessimism of modern nihilism have all challenged the traditional ideas of life after death. They also challenge the idea of any transcending meaning in life. That is, these life philosophies have questioned (or simply denied) the belief that life may have meaning that goes beyond our mortal existence. Their objections are as much about the idea of meaning and values as they are about death and afterlife. Their vision of society produces peace (in theory, at least) only because human existence has no meaning beyond the limits of physical life. They would eliminate human struggle by reducing humankind to minimal significance or purpose. What we are and how we live doesn't really matter past this life. We are stripped of any responsibility or meaning beyond life. Such a philosophy offers a costly peace, indeed.

Human culture, then, reflects these two contrasting perspectives on the idea of an afterlife. On the one hand, some basic level of human awareness senses something beyond death. On the other hand, the modern rationalist questions, and attempts to avoid, the burden of responsibility and meaning that the belief in an afterlife brings with it. Clearly we struggle with an answer to the question of what awaits us after death.

Final Judgment

The Christian view, uncomfortable or not, is that there is going to be a division between persons after death. Jesus gives us a graphic portrayal of a kingly judgment that will separate the "sheep" from the "goats," the faithful from the unfaithful (Matthew 25:31-46). The notions of separation and judgment are inescapably biblical. This does not, however, reduce our faith to a primitive, punitive understanding of God's designs for us. We misunderstand the idea of judgment (and the feared condemnation that may accompany it) if we see it only as an instrument for divine punishment. The belief in judgment simply affirms the Christian understanding that the decisions and actions of our lives have eternal significance. We believe that what happens *during* our lives has meaning *beyond* our lives. God has granted us the awesome power to affect reality far beyond the limits of our mortal existence.

The idea of judgment is an expression of that personal empowerment. In giving us the power to affect our eternal destiny, God affirms our personhood and our freedom. Avoidance of judgment removes from us the dignity and power to affect our eternal destiny. The reality of judgment is not only an expression of God's wrath toward sin but also an expression about our gift of freedom and how we exercise it. In the end there will be two kinds of people—those who allow God to do with them what *He* wants and those that God allows to do what *they* want.

Heaven

Jesus often refers to "heaven" and the "kingdom of heaven" but doesn't answer every question we can pose. He tells us that He is preparing a "place" (John 14:1-4). It is a place where our "treasures" are secure (Matthew 6:20). There will be a celebration there, a wedding party (22:10-14). Jesus also refers to "paradise," a restoration to a new Garden of Eden beyond death (Luke 23:43 and Revelation 2:7). Scripture most often refers to heaven without elaboration of what it will be like.

Revelation has the most graphic details. In chapters 21 and 22 the New Jerusalem is described as having walls of jasper and covered with all sorts of precious stones. The gates are pearl, and the streets are pure gold. The river of the water of life flows through the center of the city. What an overwhelming spectacle!

It should not be surprising that Scripture does not give a comprehensive description of life in heaven. It is beyond our ability to know or comprehend. Even the powerful visual images of heavenly life in John's Revelation only portray the most wonderful life imaginable, point beyond it, and say, "Heaven is unspeakably more than this."

We can know for certain that, whatever or wherever heaven is, it is glorious existence in the presence and worship of God.

Hell

If heaven is a finally indescribable picture of joy and blessing, then hell is an equally indescribable experience of sadness and personal torment. The fact that we have chosen separation from God and His blessings will not mitigate the tragedy of such an existence. Scripture offers several pictures of such a state of being. One of those pictures is the Greek word Gehenna (Matthew 18:9). It is drawn from the Valley of Hinnom outside Jerusalem. This was the place where human children were offered as sacrifices by fire to the god Molech (2 Kings 23:10; 2 Chronicles 28:3; 33:6; Jeremiah 7:31; 32:35). This accursed place later became the festering garbage and dung heap of Jerusalem. It was a place of decay and ceaseless burning as the refuse consumed itself. A more distasteful and unpleasant image could hardly be found in the biblical world.

A second image of the afterlife apart from God's presence is Hades (Matthew 11:23, margin; 16:18; Revelation 20:13-14). Hades, the Greek word for the afterworld, came to serve as a translation of the Old Testament Hebrew name for the afterworld, "Sheol." Hades portrays a shadowy existence of individual dissolution and perpetual thirst. Its particular form of torment is the deprivation of personal substance and significance. Hades reveals the illusion of man's self-sufficiency in sustaining life without God.

Such images of human torment and loss can only begin to portray existence separated from God. We can hardly begin to imagine life without the life, grace, and love-giving presence of the Spirit of God.

This present world's worst nightmares are only a pale shadow of the full reality of existence apart from God. The madness of urban riots in America, the horrors of genocide in Africa, and the deep-seated hatred and cruelty in the Balkans of Europe are only dark shadows of a more terrifying reality. Just try to picture the crowded cities of the world with the restraining and redemptive presence of God's Spirit totally withdrawn. The most base human desires or behaviors would replace the last vestiges of compassion, kindness, or mercy. We can hardly begin to imagine such a living nightmare. Hell's portrayals are a limited description of the most anguished and empty kind of existence we can envision. Scripture points to those images and says, "Hell is unspeakably worse."

A Christian Perspective

Judgment, heaven, and hell relate to the meaning and significance of human life and choice. These issues define the scope of the humanity that God has granted to us. They express the extent of the power that God has given to us. They declare that God has given to us the freedom to choose whether we would rather rule in hell than serve in heaven. If the awesome sweep of that vision frightens us, it may also lift us and give us hope and encouragement. God has made it possible for us to choose the great blessedness. Though our natural choices would destine us for separation from God, He has made possible our restoration—though it was costly. No other remedy could restore the hope of paradise to us than the sacrificial life and death of God's only Son. No one else could pay the price. No one else could reopen the gates of heaven.

What good news it is to know that "God so loved the world that he gave his one and only Son, that whoever believes in him shall not perish but have eternal life" (John 3:16). Heaven is again available to us. The prospect of judgment is not the expression of God's cruelty but His weighty gift. It is the ultimate burden and opportunity of being made in the image of God.

1. Edith Hamilton, *Mythology* (New York: New American Library, 1942), 39-40.

Background Scripture: 2 Kings 23:10; 2 Chronicles 28:3; 33:6; Jeremiah 7:31; 32:35; Matthew 6:20; 11:23; 16:18; 18:9; 22:10-14; 25:31-46; Luke 23:43; John 3:16; 14:1-4; Revelation 2:7; 20:13-14; 21:1—22:21

SECTION III

The End of the World

by Roger Hahn

Roger Hahn, Ph.D., is professor of New Testament and director of the Master of Divinity program at Nazarene Theological Seminary, Kansas City.

Important Words in This Chapter

See *Glossary* for definitions.

Amillennialism

Dispensation

Dispensational premillennialism

Dispensationalism

Eschatology

Futuristic eschatology

Historic premillennialism

Inaugurated eschatology

Materialism

Messiah

Messianic

Millennium

Postmillennialism

Premillennialism

Rapture

Realized eschatology

Resurrection

Second Coming

Synoptic

Tribulation

CHAPTER 6

The Second Coming and the Kingdom of God

MY FIRST SERMON HAD THE GOAL OF STRAIGHTEN-ing the world out about the second coming of Christ. I was 19 years old. I had no training in theology or preaching. The sermon lasted seven minutes before I ran out of ammunition.

The memory of that sermon brings embarrassment now. I really knew nothing about the Second Coming. But like lots of folks at that stage of life, I thought it was the most important subject in the world.

I still believe the Second Coming is a very important subject for believers. However, over 25 years of disciplined study of the Bible has given me a larger context for understanding the topic. In the New Testament, Jesus' return is part of the larger subject—the kingdom of God.

When the Bible mentions the kingdom of God, it does not refer to a place. Rather, the kingdom of God describes a relationship between God and persons. In this relationship God is King—the absolute Ruler. People lovingly and obediently serve this King, who is God.

Understood this way, the kingdom of God has always existed in the hearts of devout believers. However, God's reign in individual lives was only a partial and preliminary step. Jesus proclaimed that the kingdom of God means total obedience to God the Father. That life of complete obedience is not to be a private matter. Rather, the kingdom of God is to be the growing company of totally obedient disciples.

To this point the Kingdom could be understood completely in the present (tense). However, even the Old Testament envisioned God's kingly rule as eternal and complete. Psalm 45:6; Daniel 2:44; and Daniel 6:26 make that clear. Since the present experiences of God's rule are only partial, the complete and perfect obedience of the Kingdom will lie in the future. The New Testament writers believed that the completion of the Kingdom would coincide with the second coming of Christ. Then "every knee should bow . . . and every tongue confess" (Philippians 2:10-11). Instead of being absolute Ruler of *some* hearts in faith, in fact God will become King of *every* living being.

Jesus' Teaching About the Kingdom

The kingdom of God is the main subject of Jesus' teaching as the Synoptic Gospels (Matthew, Mark, and Luke) present His ministry. The Gospel of John uses the language of "life" and "eternal life" to describe the same concept. Jesus' teaching built on the understandings of Jewish people in His time. To fully understand Jesus' words on the kingdom of God, we must understand the way Jews of Jesus' time thought about the end of time and the future.

During Jesus' life, Judaism believed that human history could be divided into two ages. The first was this "present, evil age." This included the past and the unfolding present. The other age was the "age to come." This was obviously in the future. It would be a time in which sin and evil would be destroyed. As such, complete obedience to God would characterize the age to come. For that reason many Jews used the expression "the kingdom of God" and the "age to come" interchangeably.

Such a dramatic change from this "present, evil age" to the "age to come" could only happen when the Messiah came. Thus some Jews referred to the "kingdom of God/age to come" as the "messianic age." The "age of the [Holy] Spirit" was another phrase used for this future time of complete obedience to God. Judaism did not believe that this change of ages would happen instantaneously. There would be a brief transition period of conflict between the good (age to come) and the evil (present age). They called this transition period "the day of the Lord" or just "the day."

Jesus began His ministry announcing, "The time has come. . . . The kingdom of God is near" (Mark 1:15). Everyone listening would have understood that the transition between the two ages was beginning. However, 20th-century scholars have disagreed about Jesus' understanding of the exact timing of the kingdom of God and His own ministry. Three views have emerged.

Present reality. In many passages, Jesus speaks of the Kingdom as a present reality. According to Luke 17:20-21, the Pharisees asked Jesus about the timing of the kingdom of God. He warned against looking for signs and said, "The kingdom of God is within you" (v. 21). Thus the transitional "day" was past, and the Kingdom was already a present reality during Jesus' ministry. Scholars call this view "realized eschatology."

Future reality. Other passages seem to present the Kingdom as a future reality. Jesus stated during the Last Supper that He would not again drink the fruit of the vine until He drank "anew in the kingdom of God" (Mark 14:25). (See also Luke 22:18.) This certainly implies that the Kingdom was still future and that Jesus looked forward to its coming. Scholars call this "consistent" or "futuristic eschatology."

Present in Jesus himself. The fact that Jesus spoke of the kingdom of God both as a present reality and as a future hope has led to another position, which asserts that Jesus brought the Kingdom as part of His ministry. In that regard, it was present in the ministry of Jesus. In fact, it was present in Jesus himself. However, Jesus' ministry began the transition period between the two ages. The completion of the

Kingdom was still in the future. Not until that future time would obedience to God become universal and the Kingdom become eternal. This idea is called "inaugurated eschatology" and fits the biblical evidence best.

Inaugurated eschatology maintains that Jesus taught that the Kingdom was both present and future. Jesus' earliest followers picked up on this and taught that the Second Coming would mark the end of the transition period. It would also mark the beginning of the full experience of the kingdom of God.

Thus the New Testament does not teach that the kingdom of God comes by human effort. It was and is the product of God's timing and His gracious gift of sending Christ (twice). The kingdom of God began at the first coming of Christ. It is a present reality in the life of the Church. It will reach its eternal fullness when Christ returns. This shows how important the Second Coming is in the whole plan of God for human history.

Millennial Views

Six times in the 20th chapter of Revelation the author refers to a 1,000-year period. Twice the author speaks of believers reigning with Christ for that length of time. Early in the history of the Church, Christians began to associate the 1,000 years of Revelation 20 with the kingdom of God. Through the course of church history four major ways of interpretation developed. We call these "millennial" views, from the Latin expression for 1,000 years.

A person can believe in the second coming of Christ without agreeing with one of the four millennial interpretations. However, these positions have been so influential that most discussion of the Second Coming is built around one of them. There are many variations within each of the four, and some people try to draw the best from each view.

Historic premillennialism. (See fig. 1.) The term "historic" distinguishes this view from the fourth one, called "dispensational premillennialism." The term "premillennial" reflects the position that Christ will return *before* the 1,000 years of Revelation 20. In fact, premillennialism asserts that the Second Coming will be the event that begins the 1,000 years.

Premillennialists also believe that Christ will return after a seven-year period of persecution or "tribulation" for the Church. When He returns, all believers who have died will be raised from the dead. The Christians who are alive and the resurrected believers will join Christ for a 1,000-year expression of the kingdom of God. During that time, Christ physically will rule on earth. For the first time in human history there will be universal political peace.

Following the 1,000 years of peace, a second resurrection will occur. At this time those who died as unbelievers will be raised and brought to judgment. At this point, time as we know it will end. Both the righteous and unbelievers will move to their eternal destiny.

Papias, who died about A.D. 130, taught certain portions of this belief. Thus premillennialists claim that their position is the oldest (and thus most accurate) Christian interpretation of the Second Coming.

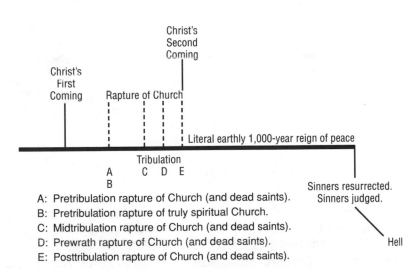

A: Pretribulation rapture of Church (and dead saints).
B: Pretribulation rapture of truly spiritual Church.
C: Midtribulation rapture of Church (and dead saints).
D: Prewrath rapture of Church (and dead saints).
E: Posttribulation rapture of Church (and dead saints).

FIGURE 1   PREMILLENNIALISM

Amillennialism. (See fig. 2.) The belief called "amillennialism" says that the 1,000 years of Revelation 20 do not refer to a literal and future period of history. Instead, the years of peace are symbolic of the present reality of the kingdom of God begun in the ministry of Jesus. Thus, the reign of Christ during the millennium is a spiritual reign over believers. The Second Coming will occur at the end of the present reality of the Kingdom, and Christ will then set up His eternal and full kingdom.

Justin Martyr, who died about A.D. 165, wrote of Christians in his time who held amillennialist opinions of the Second Coming. Premillennialist and amillennialist positions probably existed side by side from the earliest days of Christianity. However, amillennialism has been the most influential view through the whole history of Christianity. By the time of Augustine (around A.D. 400), amillennialism had become the standard interpretation of the Second Coming in Christianity. That would remain true until the 19th century.

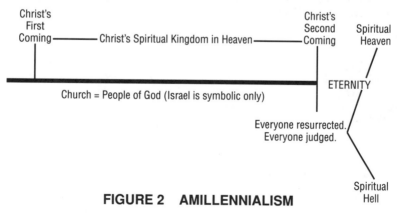

FIGURE 2   AMILLENNIALISM

Postmillennialism. (See fig. 3.) "Postmillennialism" teaches that Christ will come *after* the 1,000 years of Revelation 20. Postmillennialists believe that the time period of Revelation should be understood as 1,000 years, but that spiritual period is still in the future. They believe God will someday so empower the proclamation of the gospel that Christianity will come to have a major influence on human history. Because of this Christian influence, war and institutional forms for evil will be abolished. Gospel preaching will be so powerful that most people will accept Christ. After 1,000 years of such peace, Christ will return, the Judgment will take place, and eternity will begin.

Postmillennialism was the most prominent during the 19th and early 20th centuries. Its optimism matched the feelings of the Age of Reason and the growth of science and medicine. Two world wars, several smaller wars, the Great Depression, and the rise of crime have caused many Christians to abandon postmillennialism. However, some highly respected and trustworthy Christians still hold to it.

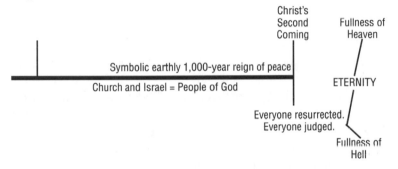

Christ's Second Coming

Fullness of Heaven

Symbolic earthly 1,000-year reign of peace

Church and Israel = People of God

ETERNITY

Everyone resurrected.
Everyone judged.

Fullness of Hell

FIGURE 3   POSTMILLENNIALISM

Dispensational premillennialism. (See fig. 1) Like historic premillennialism, this position asserts that Christ's second coming will happen before the 1,000 years of peace mentioned in Revelation 20. The term "dispensational" comes from the belief that God has divided human history into different periods or "dispensations." Persons who hold this view believe that human beings are saved in different ways in the separate dispensations. Most adherents believe in seven dispensations, though recent scholars have reduced that number to as few as two.

Dispensationalists also sharply distinguish between the Church and Israel as the people of God. Most believe that Christ will appear in the air and rapture the Church away to heaven before a seven-year period of tribulation. (They often call this the "pretribulation Rapture of the Church." As fig. 1 shows, there are several opinions about when the rapture of the Church might take place.) Following the Tribulation, the 1,000 years of peace will take place, but it will involve the nation of Israel and the Jewish people. Dispensationalists believe all the promises of the Old Testament to Israel will be literally fulfilled during this period of time. At the end of the millennium, the final Judgment will take place.

Dispensational premillennialism is the most recent interpretation to develop. Most scholars believe it began with the ministry of John Darby in Great Britain in the mid-19th century. The *Scofield Bible* notes popularized it just after the 20th century began. By the middle of the 20th century, dispensationalism was the most popular explanation of the Second Coming among evangelical believers. Since the 1960s public media have made these ideas available to wide audiences. Films such as *A Thief in the Night*, books by Hal Lindsey like *The Late Great Planet Earth*, and a multitude of TV and radio preachers are well-known examples. However, the influence of this position among Christian scholars declined a bit near the end of the 20th century.

Understanding the four millennial interpretations is necessary in sorting out the claims and counterclaims made by evangelical Christians about the Second Coming. Several of the following chapters will build on these definitions and show how the various views treat subjects related to the Second Coming differently.

The Nature and Date of the Second Coming

Reading about all the differences in the opinions on the Second Coming can lead a person to think that Christians do not agree about anything regarding the subject. That is not true. All evangelical Christians believe that Christ's second coming will be *personal* and *visible*. That means that we believe Jesus himself will appear in a visible form. The Second Coming should not be confused with the spiritual coming of Christ into a person's heart. We do not look for a ghost or a spirit. We expect to be able to see and touch Christ when He returns.

All Christians also believe that Christ's return will be *sudden* and *unexpected*. The parable of the 10 virgins tells us that some will be prepared and some will not be prepared for that event. However, there is disagreement about how sudden and how unexpected the Second Coming will be. Many believers think that there are "signs of the times" (Matthew 16:3) that tell us that Christ's return will be very soon. Others believe that those "signs" have been present since Christ's first coming. They emphasize the Scriptures that tell us that no one except God the Father knows the date or the time of the Second Coming (Matthew 24:36). This warns that trying to guess the date is not the job of Christians.

Unfortunately, many modern Christians think of the Second Coming with fear. Our materialism and the occasional use of scare-tactics evangelism have contributed to this. The New Testament always sees the Second Coming as a wonderful event. Titus 2:13 calls it our "blessed hope." Paul tells the Thessalonians to "encourage each other" with his teaching about the Second Coming (1 Thessalonians 4:18). May God help us recapture the optimism and joy the New Testament Church felt about the second coming of Christ.

Background Scripture: Psalm 45:6; Daniel 2:44; 6:26; Matthew 16:3; 24:36; Mark 1:15; 14:25; Luke 17:20-21; 22:18; Philippians 2:10-11; 1 Thessalonians 4:18; Titus 2:13; Revelation 20

Important Words in This Chapter

See *Glossary* for definitions.

Calvinism

Dispensationalism

Postmillennialism

Premillennialism

Prophecy

Resurrection

Second Coming

Wesleyan

CHAPTER 7

What Do Wesleyans* Believe?

AT ONE TIME FIVE FAMILIES FROM MY SIBLINGS AND in-laws owned minivans. Yet there was no duplication of model or style of any of the five minivans. The family agreed considerably on the usefulness and value of such a vehicle. Yet a great deal of disagreement occurred about the specific features and models. Frequently somebody's van would receive this response: "I wouldn't own a [certain brand] minivan if they gave it to me." The speaker would then give a spirited defense of the model and style he or she especially liked. Our family experienced general agreement on the value of minivans. However, we had major disagreements when it came to details.

A similar situation is true regarding Christian faith in the second coming of Christ. Evangelical Christians generally agree that Christ will return personally, visibly, and unexpectedly. Nevertheless, when it comes to the details, there is major disagreement. The four millennial views explained in chapter 6 all have many subgroups who strongly disagree with each other. Yet it is clear to any outside observer that all are evangelical Christians.

*The word "Wesleyan" here refers to those who follow the theological teachings of John Wesley, not only the members of The Wesleyan Church.

Disagreement about details of the Second Coming does not dechristianize a believer.

The same is true about Wesleyans and their beliefs regarding the Second Coming. All Wesleyans agree that Christ will return. But when it comes to the details of how and when that will happen, there are wide varieties of opinions. The influence of the various millennial theories has varied through the history of the Wesleyan movement. Even today there are defenders of all four millennial theories who consider themselves Wesleyans.

This does not mean that Wesleyans are identical to other evangelicals regarding the Second Coming. Wesleyans tend to view the Second Coming as a less urgent subject than personal relationship with Christ. This emphasis on salvation and sanctification shapes Wesleyan theology more than our millennial theories. For us the crucial point is always the question of what salvation in all its fullness means.

Wesleyan Views in the Past

John Wesley was interested in last things. The desire to "flee from the wrath to come" (Matthew 3:7, KJV) motivated much of his personal discipline. The desire to save others from the coming Judgment motivated his ministry.

Many scholars believe that Wesley was a premillennialist. He wrote with appreciation of several authors who were premillennial. The Revelation section of his *Explanatory Notes upon the New Testament* relies almost completely on the work of Johann Bengel. Bengel taught a type of premillennialism. Wesley's notes on other passages of the New Testament, however, lead other scholars to conclude that he was a postmillennialist.

Wesley's interest in end times did not lead him to speculate about dates. Though he appreciated the work of some premillennialists, he did not endorse their views. In 1788 he was accused of setting a date for the end of the world. His letter of reply reveals Wesley's focus: "I said nothing, less or more, in Bradford church, concerning the end of the world . . . [What I said was] that Bengelius had given it as his opinion . . . I have no opinion at all upon [that topic]: I can determine nothing at all about it. . . . I have only one thing to do,—to save my soul, and those that hear me."[1] These words capture the Wesleyan spirit that the last things are important and interesting but that personal relationship with Christ is central.

Following Wesley's death, the Wesleyan movement expanded most rapidly in America. There Wesleyans encountered the rising tide of postmillennialism. Phoebe Palmer was a major lay leader in the 19th-century Wesleyan movement. She adopted a form of postmillennialism. She wrote several letters scolding William Miller, the premillennialist, who had predicted the Second Coming would be in 1843. Such date setting was unscriptural, according to Palmer. She also thought it distracted from the central work of the Church: winning people to Christ.

Daniel Steele was one of the most respected scholars of the Wesleyan movement at the end of the 19th century. He wrote a vigorous defense of postmillennialism. He especially rejected the emerging dispensational premillennialism taught by John Darby. For a time Wesleyans contended that dispensationalism was Calvinistic. As a result it was not until the turn of the 20th century that premillennialism began to make significant inroads into Wesleyan circles.

The 20th century witnessed a reluctant tolerance of millennial views among Wesleyans. In 1932 A. M. Hills published his systematic theology, which contained his postmillennial views. In the volume he included a defense of premillennialism written by J. B. Chapman, a general superintendent in the Church of the Nazarene. Hills invited his readers to study both views and form their own "intelligent opinion."[2]

An incident in my own educational journey illustrates the Wesleyan freedom regarding views of the end times. The issue of millennial views came up in a college class on my denomination's history. The instructor reviewed the millennial theories and pointed out the variety of positions taken by church leaders throughout our history. Then he concluded, "Really, most of us are 'panmillennialists.' We believe it will all pan out in the end." Such good humor characterizes the Wesleyan emphasis that God is the only One who knows exactly how the end will happen.

Wesleyan Distinctives

The differences of opinions about the Second Coming do not mean that Wesleyans are uninterested in the end times. Friendly tolerance about the details is common. Yet, all Wesleyans share certain core beliefs regarding last things.

Most denominations state their official theology in a series of paragraphs called "Articles of Faith" or "Articles of Religion." Comparing the official end-time theology of three major Wesleyan-Holiness denominations shows striking similarities. The Church of the Nazarene, the Free Methodist Church, and The Wesleyan Church all have paragraphs on the Second Coming, resurrection, Judgment, and eternal destiny in their official statements of faith.[3] (See Appendix 1.) The statements on end times of these three denominations are cited by the eminent Methodist scholar, Thomas Oden, as representative of the views of the Wesleyan tradition.[4]

What do these official statements say Wesleyan Christians believe about the Second Coming? We believe that Christ's return is certain and that it could happen at any time. When Christ returns, all prophecy regarding the end of time will be fulfilled, though Wesleyans do not predict how that will happen. The coming of Christ should not cause fear but joyful anticipation. However, we do not simply regard the Second Coming in terms of what it will do for us personally. Rather, the certainty of Christ's return should motivate us to holy living and active evangelism.

Wesleyans also affirm the resurrection of the dead in connection with the Second Coming. Most do not state the exact timing of the resurrection compared to the Second Coming, as some other theological traditions do. Some Wesleyans specify that the resurrection of the righteous will happen at the time of the Second Coming, and the resurrection of the wicked will occur later. Most simply affirm that both just and unjust will be raised to be judged by God.

It is interesting and important to note that the doctrinal statements of these three main Wesleyan denominations affirm that the Bible teaches that the body is significant and that death marks the end of human life. Our hope and faith are that God will raise us from the dead and give us a spiritual body. Because it is a body, a person will be recognizable and whole. Because it is spiritual, we do not know exactly how it will differ from our physical bodies.

All Wesleyans believe in a future judgment following the Second Coming. God will be the Judge. Every person, whether righteous or wicked, will appear before God. He will judge fairly according to the life each person has lived and the decisions each one has made regarding the gospel. The righteous will receive their final rewards, and the wicked will receive their final punishments as a result of the Judgment.

All Wesleyans believe in a final destiny for every person. Those who are judged righteous by the gospel at the Judgment will enjoy the glories of heaven. Eternity in the presence of Christ is the chief blessing of heaven. The unrepentant will experience the eternal suffering of hell. Separation from God is hell's greatest torment.

These affirmations of faith in the Second Coming, resurrection, Judgment, and final destiny identify Wesleyans as part of the main stream of historic, orthodox Christian faith. The Wesleyan practice of not speculating about the order of events at the end time is not a sign of doctrinal softness. Only people who are unaware of church history would call Wesleyans "liberal" for failing to require belief in a particular millennial view.

Millennial views have changed greatly in their degree of influence throughout church history. They will continue to do so. My seminary theology teacher taught premillennialism throughout most of his life. Near his retirement he decided he had been wrong. He declared that he had become "a desk-pounding postmillennialist." Did he become less of a Wesleyan when he changed his mind? Of course not! Did he become a better Christian? Probably not. We could debate whether he was right or wrong in his decision, but there was no question about his relationship to Christ.

Implications of the Wesleyan Approach

There are several important implications arising from the Wesleyan way of thinking about end times. First, Wesleyans are more interested in a person's present relationship with God than we are in information about the future of human history. Knowing the exact date of the Second Coming and the "correct" millennial view will not save a person at the Last Judgment. Salvation is by faith, and Romans 10:17 states that "faith comes from hearing the message, and the message is heard through the word of Christ." Thus evangelism and missions are more important for Wesleyans than prophecy conferences. Ethics and a daily devotion of holy living are more important than charts.

Another important implication of the Wesleyan approach to last things is confidence that God can still work in the world. The more radical forms of dispensationalism are very pessimistic. Its followers believe there is no hope for the world. They say Christians must withdraw from the world so they will not be influenced toward wickedness. Wesleyans do not agree with such a view. We believe God can bring good on earth through the efforts of dedicated believers. God can use us to reduce the influence of evil and to make the world a better place. Thus, Wesleyans are involved in compassionate ministries and issues of social justice. No matter what view we hold, we do believe it is Kingdom work to fight against evil.

The Wesleyan optimism that God still wants to accomplish good in the world in which we live has another implication. The biblical message of the end times is part of the gospel. It is good news. That means that we must present this message in a way that invites people to Christ rather than scaring them to a response. John Wesley himself said that the message of holy living must be presented "drawingly." Our evangelism must never be understood simply as, "Make a trip to the altar so you won't go to hell." Our message is always, "Come and discover the fullness of life that Christ has for you."

When we respond to that invitation, we find real life here and can enjoy eternal life in the hereafter.

1. John Wesley, *The Works of John Wesley*, 3rd ed., 14 vols. (reprint; Kansas City: Beacon Hill Press of Kansas City, 1978-79),12:319.

2. A. M. Hills, *Fundamental Christian Theology* (Pasadena, Calif.: C. J. Kinne, 1932), 550.

3. These statements can be found in the *Manual: Church of the Nazarene*, the *Book of Discipline* of the Free Methodist Church, and the *Discipline of the Wesleyan Church*.

4. Thomas C. Oden, *Doctrinal Standards in the Wesleyan Tradition* (Grand Rapids: Francis Asbury Press, 1988), 159-61.

Background Scripture: Matthew 3:7; Romans 10:17

Important Words in This Chapter

See *Glossary* for definitions.

Apocalypse

Apocalyptic

Completed apocalyptic

Dead Sea Scrolls

Futurist apocalyptic

Historical apocalyptic

Prophecy

Symbolic apocalyptic

CHAPTER 8

How Do We Read the Bible?

I WAS RECENTLY TALKING WITH AN ACQUAINTANCE. He was clearly concerned about something. I sensed he wanted my opinion, but it took awhile for him to gather his courage. Finally he blurted out, "A friend of mine got a check the other day. You know what? The number up on the corner of the check was 666! Do you think he should have cashed it? I wouldn't have."

"I'd cash it in a minute," I replied. "I don't worry about things like that."

"Boy, I do," he said, almost breathlessly. "They really bother me."

What is it about "666," the "beast," and "the Antichrist" that stirs such fear and disagreement? Why is it that Revelation is always the book people want to study most when the opportunity for Bible study is presented? Why are the mysteries of the end times so mysterious?

The answers to these questions lie in the way certain portions of the Bible were written and the way we interpret them. A correct understanding of prophecy and apocalyptic literature will go a long way in helping us answer such questions.

Prophecy and Apocalyptic Distinguished

Many think of the Bible as consisting mostly of prophecy and history. For them, Isaiah through Malachi in the Old Testament and the Book of Revelation in the New are the books of prophecy. They assume that most of the prophecy of the Bible deals with the second coming of Christ. This view does not fit the actual material we find in those books of the Bible.

We normally label all the Old Testament books from Isaiah to Daniel as prophecy. The Jews of Jesus' time did not identify these books the same way. They did not list the Book of Daniel as prophecy. Rather, they listed it under the category "Writings" along with Psalms, Job, Ruth, 1 and 2 Chronicles, and other books. Further, Jews of Jesus' time included Joshua, Judges, 1 and 2 Samuel, and 1 and 2 Kings as prophecy. This shows that the original understanding of prophecy does not match what we often think about prophecy.

Most of the books that the Jews called prophecy did not predict the future. In fact, we consider Joshua, Judges, 1 and 2 Samuel, and 1 and 2 Kings to be historical books. However, those books all share a specific theological view of history. They tell us that when Israel obeyed God, their history turned out fine. When Israel disobeyed God, their history turned sour. The other books Jews consider prophecy (Isaiah through Malachi, except Daniel) share that viewpoint about history. The main message of the prophets was, "Obey God, and enjoy peace and success. Disobey God, and the nation will be destroyed."

The prophets were mostly optimistic. They believed Israel could choose to obey God and be blessed. That is why they preached—to urge the nation to make that choice. The prophets also believed that the good things God wanted to accomplish for His people could happen as a result of their obedience through the flow of historical events. That is, people's choices would determine how the flow of history would go, whether for good or for bad.

Certain portions of the Bible do not share the optimism that the prophets normally expressed. These passages are pessimistic about human choices for the good. They conclude that humans will never choose to obey God consistently. The only way God's will for the future can happen is by His own direct intervention in history. These portions declare that He will intervene and change the flow of human history. Such material is called an "apocalypse." Bible scholars use the term "apocalyptic" to describe these sections.

Apocalyptic material can be found in some passages of the prophetic books. Isaiah, Ezekiel, and Zechariah have several chapters that fit the label. Most of the Book of Daniel is apocalyptic. Some scholars also categorize Matthew 24—25, Mark 13, and Luke 21 as apocalyptic. Apocalyptic phrases are in the New Testament letters, and much of the Book of Revelation has apocalyptic features.

When we pay attention to the difference between apocalyptic sections and prophetic sections of the Bible, an interesting result occurs. Almost all the passages traditionally interpreted as "end times" passages appear in apocalyptic sections, not in the prophetic sections.

The Nature of Apocalyptic Literature

The discovery of the Dead Sea Scrolls reminded Christianity that the events, movements, and writings of Judaism at the time of Jesus are very important for understanding the Bible. When looking at Jewish writings between the Old and New Testaments, we discover that much more apocalyptic material was written than appears in the Bible. Study of such Jewish apocalyptic writing helps us understand what the biblical authors were trying to communicate in such material.

Apocalyptic writings express confidence that God can still fix what has gone wrong with the world even when there is no hope of human circumstances improving. Most apocalyptic material was written when God's people were being persecuted by an evil government. They saw no hope that circumstances would ever get better. Prayer, obedience, and proclamation of God's truth had all failed to bring down the evil ruler. Apocalyptic writers try to communicate the hope that God will enter human history, destroy the evil power structures, and restore His people.

Obviously such a message would be politically dangerous. An evil government would not tolerate people writing messages about its own downfall at the hands of God. As a result, apocalyptic literature is written in code. Stories with visions, animals, colors, and even numbers are used in symbolic ways. God's people would know what ruler the dragon represented, but the ruler would not understand. Apocalyptic writing allowed God's people to encourage one another that the Lord was about to destroy the evil powers persecuting them without those enemies knowing the message and punishing them for it.

Implications for Our Understanding

These facts reveal several implications about apocalyptic literature. First, the fact that this literature was written in code means that it is very difficult to interpret without the code, resulting in great disagreement about millennial theories and end-time ideas. Each chart maker and expert in Bible prophecy claims to have found the key. The many disagreements make it hard for us to believe that they really have. In fact, we should probably be suspicious of anyone who claims to understand all the prophecies (apocalyptic passages) of the Bible.

We often overlook a second implication. The apocalyptic passages were written to encourage the people at the time the author was writing. We must interpret this literature in a way that would have made sense to the original readers and listeners. When people claim interpretations limited only to our century, they imply that the Bible made no sense to people when it was written or anytime until our generation. Clearly the Bible would have made sense to the first readers. In all other kinds of literature in the Bible we assume that the author was trying to communicate clearly to his original readers. Why should we assume something different about an apocalypse?

A third implication that we often forget is that an apocalypse was written for encouragement. Some people conclude that if we cannot know the code, and the apocalyptic material was written to make sense to the first readers, then all important meaning is taken away. That is not true. Though we may not understand all the symbols, we know the purpose. These passages of scripture were written to encourage God's people that He was still on the throne. The message is clear— God wins in the end. That message is vitally important in our day also. We do not have to have all the information about the meaning of 666 or the dragon to receive a clear word from God.

A final implication is that we must respect the symbolism used by the original author as symbolism. Some people loudly claim that their interpretation of apocalyptic material is correct because they interpret the Bible literally. It is no virtue to interpret a Bible passage literally when the author intended for it to be understood symbolically. Most of us understand that. For example, in Psalm 18:2 the psalmist writes, "The LORD is my rock, my fortress . . . my shield and the horn of my salvation." We recognize the figures of speech and interpret them figuratively.

Biblical authors used the language, the symbolism, and the figures of speech that communicated in the culture of their day. We must find the heart of the author's original meaning rather than becoming bogged down in the details of ancient language.

Interpreting the Book of Revelation and Other Apocalyptic Material

Throughout the history of Christianity four major ways of interpreting the Book of Revelation have been developed. These approaches accurately describe the different ways we can look at apocalyptic literature.

Historical: The historical approach has seen Revelation as the history of the Christian church from beginning to end written in advance. The interpreters following this approach try to identify the various ages of church history with different sections of Revelation and other apocalyptic material. The problem with this view is that it keeps changing as church history continues unfolding.

Futurist: The futurist approach believes that the purpose of Revelation is to predict the end of time in the future. Futurist interpreters have had a hard time explaining how apocalyptic literature could be understood by the original readers.

Symbolic: The symbolic approach ignores the specific circumstances when Revelation was written. This system of interpretation sees the symbolism of apocalyptic literature as designed to express universal and abstract theological truths. This view also fails to take the original audience and circumstances seriously.

Completed*: This approach attempts to place all the meaning in the time and circumstances of the original readers. Thus, the total meaning of the Book of Revelation would be found in the events of the first-century Church. While this is an important starting point, it fails to exhaust the meaning of apocalyptic literature.

We need a method that draws on the strengths of these approaches and avoids the weaknesses of each. This means that a combination of approaches will be necessary. The starting point of all interpretation of the Bible is the original intention of the author to communicate with readers.

Thus, interpretation of the apocalyptic sections of the Bible should start with the circumstances of the original readers. This means that we take seriously the fact that apocalyptic writing uses symbolic rather than literal language. From the symbolism and circumstances we determine the spiritual message the author wanted to communicate. Finally, we ap-

---

*Scholars call this the "preterist" method.

ply that spiritual message to the needs and circumstances of today.

What can we expect from such an approach? It will tell us that human history as we know it will someday end. That the end of time will be associated with the second coming of Christ. What we are talking about is not an individual's death, but a cataclysmic change that will affect the whole universe.

The Bible indicates that Christ's coming will be sudden and unexpected. From the perspective of a sinful world, the end of human existence as we have known it will be a catastrophe. For believers it will be the climactic fulfillment of our hope that God will finally make all things right. For that reason we look forward to the end of time joyfully and hopefully.

Background Scripture: Psalm 18:2; Matthew 24—25; Mark 13; Luke 21

IMPORTANT WORDS IN THIS CHAPTER

See *Glossary* for definitions.

Amillennialism

Anti-Semitism

Armageddon

Dispensational premillennialism

Dispensationalism

Eschatology

Figurative language

Gentiles

Gog

Historic premillennialism

Prophecy

Synagogue

Tribulation

Zionism

CHAPTER 9

What About Israel?

DURING THE FALL OF 1990 AND THE BEGINNING OF 1991, worldwide attention was drawn to the Middle East. The Iraqi invasion of Kuwait and the opposing buildup of a multinational force led by the United States sparked heated discussions about what might happen. Considerable concern arose whether Israel would be drawn into the conflict or whether Israel could be kept out of it. Christians found themselves divided over the question of whether the events surrounding the Gulf War had significance for biblical prophecy and the end of time.

I heard a pastor preach a series of sermons on Babylon, Israel, and end-time prophecies. After one of the sermons, I heard a person in the foyer remarking, "This is the best preaching our pastor has ever done!" However, I also discovered others who thought the opposite.

The question of the role of the Middle East, especially Israel, in biblical prophecy is quite controversial. Neither the quick end to the Gulf War nor the ongoing military and political tensions of the area help resolve the question. Yet many Christians have an ongoing interest in the question: How is Israel involved in the events surrounding the Second Coming?

Israel and Dispensationalism

Some Christians make a major distinction between the Church as the people of God and Israel as the people of God. They believe Christ will take the Church to heaven before or during the Tribulation. Then the Old Testament promises will be fulfilled in a literal way to the nation of Israel. Not everyone agrees about all the details of how Israel fits into this outline. However, it is the influence of dispensationalism that made Israel an important question in terms of end times. The events in the Middle East during the 20th century have provided plenty of fuel for the lay theologians under dispensational influence. However, many end-time and millennial views see little, or a very different, significance for Israel.

The fall of Jerusalem to Babylon in 586 B.C. began the process of scattering the Jewish people around the world. Many Jews returned to their homeland in 537 B.C., but they were a minority compared to those who remained in Babylon and Egypt. Even in New Testament times more Jews lived outside the Holy Land than lived in it. The fall of Jerusalem and destruction of the second Temple in A.D. 70 and the annihilation of Jews during the Second Jewish War in A.D. 132-35 caused almost all Jews to move away from the Holy Land. Though individual Jews returned to the Holy Land at various times throughout the intervening years, no mass return took place until the 20th century.

The first wave of Jewish returnees came from Russia at the end of the 19th century. Then Jews from Great Britain and western Europe led the second wave in the early 20th century. The small trickle grew to a stream of Jews returning until the tragic program of anti-Semitism under Hitler in Nazi Germany. Following World War II, the stream became a flood. Political momentum had gathered in Britain and Western Europe to provide an independent nation of Israel. That became a reality on May 14, 1948.

The movement of Jews returning to the Holy Land (called Zionism) developed about a generation after the popularization of dispensationalism. Many Christians thought the growth and success of Zionism provided confirmation of the dispensational interpretation of prophecy. Military events bolstered the confidence that the nation of Israel was the fulfillment of prophecy in the middle of the 20th century. Four times the Arab nations surrounding Israel mounted military campaigns to "drive Israel into the sea." They hoped to destroy the independent Jewish homeland. The size of armies and numbers of weapons favored an Arab victory. The fact that Israel soundly, and usually swiftly, defeated the invaders caused previous doubters to believe that God's plan for Israel was unfolding and that the Second Coming was close at hand.

When the former Soviet Union began to support the Arab cause, some Christians pointed to all the pieces falling in place. They reasoned the Soviet Union was Gog that would come from the north, as prophesied in Ezekiel 38—39. They believed that the great battle of Armageddon mentioned in Revelation 16:16 would explode out of the Arab-Israeli conflict when the Soviet Union would intervene to help the Arabs. When Israel captured and kept East Jerusalem in 1967, speculation regarding the rebuilding of the Temple began to escalate. The Gulf War in 1991 and ongoing tensions in the Middle East have kept the interest in Israel high among many people.

The Biblical Basis for the Dispensational View

The complex nature of Scripture means that all believers must employ literal, symbolic, figurative, or spiritualized interpretations on some points, depending on the context. Dispensationalists, though, especially emphasize a literal approach to biblical passages relating to Israel. Such Christians believe that any promises of God made to the Old Testament people of Israel must someday be fulfilled for the modern nation called Israel. The possession of the land of Palestine, physical blessings, and ultimate victory over the surrounding nations are promises dispensationalists believe God is and will be granting to present-day Israel.

As a result of this system of interpretation, many expect the Temple in Jerusalem to be rebuilt someday according to the dimensions and design described in Ezekiel 40—48. Because the Church is not specifically mentioned in the Old Testament, nor in chapters 4 through 19 of the Revelation, they conclude that the Church is a parenthesis in God's larger plan for Israel. The era of the Church falls between the days when God originally worked with Israel and the time when He will finally fulfill His promises to Israel.

Some Christians read Romans 9—11 in a way that supports this view. They note that Paul states in 11:1 that God has not rejected His people. They point out that verse 25 speaks of a hardening of Israel "until the full number of the Gentiles has come in." Verse 26 declares that "all Israel will be saved." These scriptures, the return of the Jews to Palestine in the 20th century, and the successful establishment of the modern nation of Israel make it easy for many Christians to conclude that Israel is the "clock of prophecy."

The View of Israel as a Spiritual Reality

Many Christians hold that the key to correctly interpreting the Bible is to know which passages refer to the Christian Church and which passages refer to the nation of Israel. They call this distinction "rightly dividing the word of truth," using a phrase from 2 Timothy 2:15 (KJV). However, the New Testament itself does not always support this distinction between the Church and the nation of Israel.

In Romans 9:6-7 the apostle Paul states, "For not all who are descended from Israel are Israel. Nor because they are his descendants are they all Abraham's children." Paul's point was that simply being a member of the Jewish nation does not guarantee that God's promises to Israel will apply to that person. Romans 2:28-29 defines a Jew with a spiritual definition rather than a national or ethnic definition: "A man is not a Jew if he is only one outwardly, nor is circumcision merely outward and physical. No, a man is a Jew if he is one inwardly; and circumcision is circumcision of the heart, by the Spirit, not by the written code." Paul's development of this principle implies that he considered Gentiles who believed in Christ to be more authentically Jewish than his Jewish countrymen who rejected their Messiah.

Romans 9:25-26 quotes the Old Testament, referring to Hosea 1:9-10 and 2:23. The prophecies of Hosea clearly applied to Israel the nation. Paul, just as clearly, applies them to the Church, consisting primarily of Gentiles. Thus, Paul establishes a New Testament pattern of interpreting Old Testament passages about Israel as fulfilled in the Church. Many conservative evangelicals can point to the apostle Paul to support a spiritual rather than literal interpretation of Israel. The dispensational claim that all God's promises to Israel in the Old Testament must be fulfilled to the Jewish nation may be true. However, many New Testament passages suggest that Christians have inherited the promises of the Old Testament to Israel.

People who interpret New Testament references to Israel in the spiritual sense also point to the hostility toward Christianity in Israel. The present spiritual condition of the nation of Israel does not match a literal interpretation of New Testament passages about Israel. Romans 11:26 declares, "All Israel will be saved." Its context seems to imply that Israel will be saved by faith in Christ. There does not appear to be one plan of salvation for Christians and another plan of salvation for Jews. Unfortunately, the modern nation of Israel has been characterized by spiritual insensitivity. Christian evangelism is prohibited by law in Israel. Further, the influential majority of Jews in Israel are atheistic or thoroughly secular. Many scholars who take the Bible seriously say that Israel can play no role in Bible prophecy until the nation accepts Christ.

The spiritual interpretation of Israel as the Church is most prominent among advocates of amillennialism. However, many followers of historic premillennialism do not attach the same significance to current political events as do adherents of dispensational premillennialism.

So What Should We Believe?

What we believe about the role of Israel in biblical prophecy must arise from personal conviction and study. It cannot be the product of a theological label that we wear. Some Wesleyans fully accept the dispensational view of Israel. There are many amillennial evangelicals (including many Wesleyans) who spiritually apply to the Church most biblical references to Israel.

Many people seek a middle way between the dispensational and the spiritual interpretations of the role of Israel in biblical prophecy. One way of doing so involves a principle developed in the Old Testament itself. There a spiritual remnant came to represent Israel. The clearest passages are in Isaiah 10:19-22; 11:11, 16. Extending this principle to the New Testament, one can see the prophecies relating to Israel being fulfilled by Jewish people, but only by those who come to faith in Christ.

Interpreting Israel geographically is another way in which some scholars seek a middle ground, because many Christians are not ready to dismiss the events of the Middle East as meaningless in God's plans for the end of time. This view interprets the prophecies that speak of Israel to apply to the *land* of Israel rather than the *nation* of Israel. From this perspective, Armageddon will indeed be the site of the final battle of history.

The way people interpret biblical prophecies about Israel is more complex than a simple choice between literal and spiritual views of Israel. Much more is at stake than whether one side or the other is "right." For example, how Americans ask the United States government to support the state of Israel is affected by the way in which many Christians view biblical prophecies concerning Israel. Support for evangelism among Arabs in Israel and the entire Middle East is influenced by particular views on Israel. Opinions about terrorism and radical political activities of Muslim Arabs are often inconsistent with opinions about similar terrorism and radical activism by Jews. Many people hold anti-Semitic views about Jews in their neighborhood and yet proclaim that God has chosen the nation of Israel to play the key role in eschatology.

The question of Israel is complex and difficult. Christians may never completely agree with each other on this area of interpretation. However, we can all join the psalmist in praying for the peace of Jerusalem (122:6).

Background Scripture: Psalm 122:6; Isaiah 10:19-22; 11:11, 16; Ezekiel 38—39; 40—48; Hosea 1:9-10; 2:23; Romans 2:28-29; 9—11; 2 Timothy 2:15; Revelation 16:16

IMPORTANT WORDS IN THIS CHAPTER

See *Glossary* for definitions.

Abomination of desolation

Amillennialism

Antiochus IV

Dispensationalism

Domitian

Gaius (Caligula)

Historic Premillennialism

Nero

Postmillennialism

Second Coming

Synoptic

Tribulation

CHAPTER 10

The Antichrist, Tribulation, and Other Scary Subjects

I HEARD THEM TALKING IN THE HALLWAY OUTSIDE my faculty office door. They were students at the Christian college where I taught.

"Have you been to the church up on Council Road?" asked one. "I went last night, and it was the scariest sermon I've ever heard!"

"No, but I bet it wasn't as scary as the guy up in Edmond," responded the other. "He talked about the beast, Iraq, and Russia. It was twice as scary as the one we went to last week in Yukon."

The young ladies walked down the hall and out of my hearing, but their conversation was not unusual. One of the popular things that semester among a group of students was to visit various, mostly nondenominational, churches and listen to sermons about the Second Coming. The goal was to see which preacher had the most frightening sermon about the end of time. One student described the process as a "Christian form of horror movies."

91

I doubt the appropriateness of the notion of a "Christian form of horror movies." However, much of the preaching on the Second Coming plays on the emotion of fear, especially fear of the unknown. Terms like "the Antichrist," "the mark of the beast," and "the Tribulation" are tossed about like emotional grenades. Many people live with dread of Christ's return because of such words. Understanding them in their biblical context can greatly reduce anxiety by increasing joyful anticipation of the Second Coming.

The Antichrist

The list of nominees for the Antichrist reads like a Who's Who of notoriously evil people. Nero, Mussolini, Hitler, Stalin, and Saddam Hussein have all been acclaimed as the Antichrist. People with a less notorious reputation, but who were powerful and influential, have also been described as the Antichrist. Many popes throughout Christian history, John F. Kennedy, and Henry Kissinger have been given the title. Such a variety of opinions suggests that the Bible's teachings about the Antichrist are easily misunderstood.

The actual word "antichrist" only appears four times in the Bible, all in the Epistles of 1 and 2 John. The plural form, "antichrists," appears once in 1 John 2:18. The main point of these passages in 1 and 2 John is that antichrist denies an important truth about Christ. In 2 John 7 and 1 John 4:3, denying that Jesus came in the flesh makes one *anti*christ (or against Christ). Denying God the Father, God the Son, and that Jesus is the Messiah are marks of the antichrist, according to 1 John 2:22. Though 1 John 2:18 connects the Antichrist with the end of time, the verse also states that many antichrists exist. In fact, anyone who denies that Jesus came in the flesh qualifies as "the antichrist," according to 2 John 7.

The impression of these passages is not that the Antichrist is some mysterious figure. Nor do we need to identify that figure so that we know the Second Coming is near. Rather, antichrist is an attitude or spirit that rejects the truth about Christ. First John 4:3 speaks of the spirit of antichrist as any spirit that does not confess the deity of Christ. The antichrist of John's letters could be any and every sinner who has secular and atheistic views of Christ. However, context of the letters implies that these people were part of the Church and teaching false doctrines about Christ.

The idea of the Antichrist, however, is built on something more than just the Bible's use of the word. Several New Testament passages imply that opposition to Christ will be personified in some terrible being before the end of time. Second Thessalonians 2:3 mentions a "man of lawlessness." Paul further describes this person as an opposer and one who exalts himself above all other beings and powers. The "man of lawlessness" will even call himself God and seat himself in the Temple of God (v. 4). This outburst of sinful arrogance will take place before the Second Coming, according to verse 3. When Christ returns, He will annihilate the "man of lawlessness" with "the breath of his mouth" (v. 8).

A few days before His crucifixion, Jesus instructed the disciples about the future. His teaching, sometimes called the Synoptic Apocalypse, appears in Matthew 24, Mark 13, and Luke 21. Several times He spoke of false prophets and people claiming to be the Messiah. However, Matthew 24:15 and Mark 13:14 speak of the "abomination of desolation" (KJV). This expression is often taken to refer to a person. Many writers associate it with the Antichrist.

Many interpreters also find the Antichrist in Revelation 13. Two beasts are described joining themselves to the dragon and persecuting the saints. The first beast comes out of the sea and has 10 horns and 7 heads. It enticed the whole earth to worship the dragon and itself. The second beast rose from the earth with two horns. It spoke like the dragon and caused people to worship the first beast. This second beast also is the one who puts his mark (the "mark of the beast") on the hand or forehead of all who wish to buy and sell. The mark is the name or the number of the beast, which verse 18 identifies as 666.

Revelation 12:9 identifies the dragon as Satan. The purpose of the beasts is to cause the whole earth to worship Satan or the first beast, who also represents Satan. The two beasts are antichrist in the sense of opposing Christ by promoting Satan. Many scholars believe the dragon (Satan) and the two beasts are a symbolic anti-Trinity. As Satan, the dragon is the opposite of God. The first beast was the opposite of Christ, and the second beast the anti-Holy Spirit. If such a view is correct, the first beast is the Antichrist.

The New Testament describes the beasts of Revelation 13, the "man of lawlessness" of 2 Thessalonians 2, and the "abomination of desolation" in the Synoptic Apocalypse with the same language as Daniel 7—12. The "abomination that maketh desolate" is specifically mentioned in Daniel 11:31 and 12:11 (KJV). As a result, many interpreters trace the concept of the Antichrist to the Book of Daniel. The way a person interprets the Daniel passages becomes the pattern for interpreting the other antichrist passages found in the New Testament.

Those who interpret Daniel as a book of prophecy predicting the future believe the "abomination" described there is the Antichrist figure of the end of time. They then interpret the passages of 2 Thessalonians 2 and Revelation 13 in a similar way. Others view Daniel as apocalyptic literature, written to encourage God's people in a specific time and place. These interpreters believe Daniel 7—12 was written in the context of the Jewish crisis in 168-167 B.C. At that time the Syrian ruler, Antiochus IV, entered the holiest part of the Temple and desecrated it as described in Daniel. Antiochus embarked on a program to destroy Judaism. He was not antichrist in the sense of being against Jesus, since Jesus had not yet been born. However, he was against Judaism and against God. Daniel 7—12 provides a good description of Jewish history leading up to the time of Antiochus.

Those who interpret the "abomination of desolation" as a historical reference to Antiochus also tend to interpret the

New Testament passages built on Daniel 7—12 in historical terms. Many, if not all, of the statements of Jesus found in Matthew 24, Mark 13, and Luke 21 were fulfilled in the First Jewish War of A.D. 66-70. It was a terrible time of persecution of the Jewish people, including Jewish Christians, by the armies of the Roman Empire. The "man of lawlessness" of 2 Thessalonians 2 and the beasts of Revelation 13 are often understood as apocalyptic references to the Roman emperors whose policies led to persecution of both Jews and Christians. The emperor Gaius, often called Caligula, had attempted to set up a statue of himself in the Temple in Jerusalem shortly before 2 Thessalonians was written. Nero and Domitian are the two emperors most often mentioned as fulfilling the Antichrist figure of Revelation 13. Both the Hebrew and Greek languages used letters for numerals. Any name could be calculated as a number. The numeric value of Nero was 666.

Most evangelical scholars hold to a combination view. They agree that historical figures like Antiochus, Caligula, and Nero were the subjects intended by Daniel, 2 Thessalonians, and Revelation. Otherwise those books of the Bible would have made no sense to the original readers and listeners. On the other hand, opposition to God and His will have always occurred, especially at pivotal times. Thus, these scholars believe we should expect a significant outbreak of anti-Christian opposition to the faithful to happen just before the Second Coming. The antichrist passages need not be predictive in a way that would enable us to name a future person as *the* Antichrist. However, those passages reflect the reality of opposition to Christian faith that will intensify as Christ's return to earth becomes nearer.

The Tribulation

Closely associated with the antichrist concept is the Tribulation. This refers to a time of intense affliction and suffering just before the Second Coming. The term "great tribulation" is sometimes used for this period. This term comes from Matthew 24:21 and Revelation 7:14 (KJV). As would be expected from these references, the meaning of the Great Tribulation is a point of disagreement among biblical scholars.

The reference to the Great Tribulation in Matthew 24:21 is part of the Synoptic Apocalypse mentioned above. Jesus warns His disciples that great tribulation such as has never been experienced before will come at the end of time. The context speaks of "abomination of desolation" (v. 15, KJV), of time being cut short for the sake of the elect (v. 22), and of false prophets and false messiahs (vv. 23-24). The reference in Revelation 7:14 describes a multitude of people from every nation clothed in white who "have come out of the great tribulation." The immediate context does not describe the Tribulation, but some scholars see various events mentioned in Revelation 6—19 as part of the Great Tribulation.

Some Bible students also point to passages where the term "tribulation" is not used, but a similar concept appears. These passages include 2 Thessalonians 2:3; 1 Timothy 4:1; 2 Timothy 3:1-5; 2 Peter 3:3; and Jude 18. According to these passages, the Tribulation will be a time in which many Christians abandon the faith, and unrestrained wickedness will wreak havoc on society as we have known it.

Many who are loyal to dispensationalism believe that Christ will come and take the Church away with Him to heaven before the Tribulation begins. They state that this is not the Second Coming, because Christ only appears "in the air" (1 Thessalonians 4:17). Seven years of great tribulation will follow in which Israel is converted. Following the seven-year Tribulation, Christ returns in His second coming to set up the millennial reign. People who believe that Christ will take the Church away before the Tribulation are called "pre-tribulationists." There are some dispensationalists who believe that the Church will endure half of the Tribulation (three and a half years). These are often called "midtribulationists." The key question among dispensationalists is how much of the Tribulation the Church will suffer—none, part, or all. (See fig. 1 in chapter 6 of this book.)

Believers in historic premillennialism are "posttribulationists" because they believe that the Church will suffer all the Tribulation. They reject the distinction made by dispensationalists between Christ's appearing and His second coming. They point out that the warnings to endure tribulation are meaningless if the Church has already been taken away to heaven. More important is the fact that the Second Coming will not be unexpected as the New Testament teaches, if seven years prior Christ appears and the Church disappears from earth.

Followers of amillennialism and postmillennialism believe that the Bible does not envision any unusual time of affliction as part of the end times. They point out that the tribulation described in the Synoptic Apocalypse was very descriptive of the suffering experienced by Christians during the First Jewish War from A.D. 66 to 70. They also note that the Greek word translated "tribulation" in the passages just mentioned appears over 50 times. It describes pressure, persecution, trouble, affliction, and suffering. Most of its occurrences do not have any reference to end times. The Tribulation will not be different in kind at the end of time than it has been throughout Christian history. End time troubles will be more intense and more widely experienced than before, but they will be the same kind of persecution Christians have always suffered.

What If I'm Confused?

There has not been space in this chapter to present the details of the wide variety of opinions about the Antichrist, the beast, and the Tribulation. It is easy to become confused with so many different interpretations. Fortunately, we are not saved by understanding all the details, but by faith in God's grace.

The Bible is clear that Christ *will* return. It is clear that the dead will be raised, and those who are alive will be caught up to be with Christ. Scripture also warns us that no one knows the day or hour that all this will take place. It also teaches us to be prepared for Christ's coming. We do not need to know the identity of the Antichrist, the beast, or even if such beings will actually figure into the end of time. We do not need to fear the Tribulation. It may be more intense than ever before, but God is able to keep us if we are willing to be faithful and kept in His care.

We should not be frightened by images like "beasts," "antichrists," and "tribulation." Paul told the Thessalonians in 1 Thessalonians 4:18 to encourage each other with the message of Christ's return. Encouragement, not fear, is the hallmark of genuine Christian teaching about the Second Coming.

Background Scripture: Daniel 7—12; Matthew 24; Mark 13; Luke 21; 1 Thessalonians 4:17-18; 2 Thessalonians 2; 1 Timothy 4:1; 2 Timothy 3:1-5; 2 Peter 3:3; 1 John 2:18, 22; 4:3; 2 John 7; Jude 18; Revelation 7:14; 12:9; 13:1-18

IMPORTANT WORDS IN THIS CHAPTER

See *Glossary* for definitions.

Dispensationalism

Hades

Historic premillennialism

Millennium

Rapture

Resurrection

Resuscitation

CHAPTER 11

Coming out of the Grave

MY YOUNG FRIEND WAS ASHEN-FACED AS HE AL-most stumbled into my office. His eyes appeared red as if he had been crying.

"What's wrong, Bill*?" I asked, motioning him to sit.

"Prof," he said, "it's my brother. He was killed in a wreck yesterday."

Before I could express my sorrow, he continued, "Why did they have to come to the hospital?"

"Who came to the hospital?" I asked as gently as I could.

His face contorted with pain. "Those people from the church we used to attend. They came to the hospital to pray to raise him from the dead. Somehow they got into where he was. They prayed, and nothing happened. Now they're saying that it's our fault. They say if we'd had enough faith, they could have brought him back to life. Prof, what do we believe about resurrection?"

My friend needed comfort and the support of a Christian brother at that moment of his life. He needed to be reminded of the powerful hope believers have that we will experience resurrection someday. It was not the proper time to go through the details right there for him, but reviewing the

*Name has been changed.

centrality and the nature of resurrection hope in this chapter is appropriate for us.

A Basic Distinction

The Christian hope has always been the resurrection of the body. Ancient creeds—the Apostles' Creed and the Nicene Creed—affirm that we believe in the resurrection of the body. In early Christianity this statement stood in sharp contrast to the Greek idea of the immortality of the soul. Greek philosophers such as Plato believed that the human body was evil but that the "real" person was a naturally good soul that never died. When the body died, the soul was set free from its imprisonment in the evil body. The free soul returned, like a spark of divinity, to the presence of God from which it had come. Thus Greeks viewed death as good because it ended the influence of an evil body over a person.

In contrast, the New Testament saw death negatively. It was the punishment for sin. The Bible taught that the body was morally neutral and could be used for good or evil, depending on the choices a person made. At the beginning of the New Testament era, Jews had differing opinions about whether any essence of a person survived the death of the body. However, their hope was not in an immortal soul. Their hope was that God would resurrect the dead in bodily form to experience the rewards and punishments of the final Judgment.

Folk theology often confuses faith in the resurrection of the body and the immortality of the soul. The two are not mutually contradictory. That is, a person may believe in both, but they are not the same. The New Testament and the early Christian creeds define the Christian hope as the resurrection of the body.

The Basis of Resurrection Hope

The Old Testament does not teach the idea of resurrection, though a few references may be interpreted in that light. Nonbiblical Jewish writings in the period between the Old and New Testaments show that resurrection became the way Jews of that time understood their hope for life after death. However, the New Testament shows that not all Jews were in agreement on the issue of resurrection. Luke 20:27; Acts 4:1-2; and Acts 23:6-9 show that Pharisees believed in resurrection, but Sadducees did not.

Jewish teaching prepared the first Christians to believe in resurrection, but it was the resurrection of Christ that became the basis for the Christian hope. First Corinthians 15 provides the major treatment of resurrection faith: "But Christ has indeed been raised from the dead, the firstfruits of those who have fallen asleep. For since death came through a man, the resurrection of the dead comes also through a man. For as in Adam all die, so in Christ all will be made alive. But each in his own turn: Christ, the firstfruits; then, when he comes, those who belong to him [will be raised]. Then the end will come" (vv. 20-24a).

Paul has here most clearly stated the faith of the first Christians. They believed that God had raised Jesus from the dead. This means that Jesus did not swoon or go into a coma. He was dead and buried, but God raised Him from the dead. Early believers viewed this as God's victory over death (see vv. 54-57). Through the resurrection of Christ, God had broken death's powerful grip over all humanity. This meant that the power of God that raised Jesus from the dead was unleashed and ready to raise believers from the dead.

How Is Resurrection Different from Resuscitation?

Because the resurrection of Jesus is the basis of the Christian hope of resurrection, there are several unique aspects of our hope. Resurrection of the body is not simply resuscitating a corpse. The resurrection of Jesus was different from what happened to Lazarus, Jairus's daughter, Dorcas, Eutychus, the widow of Nain's son, and the boys revived by Elijah and Elisha. In each of those cases life was restored to their original body, and their life was extended. All of them eventually died (again). Jesus, however, was raised to "a new life" (Romans 6:4) to never die again.

Though we do not understand how Jesus' body was transformed into a glorified body, in 1 Corinthians 15:35-50 the apostle Paul addressed the question of what kind of body resurrected people have. He does not answer our questions about the exact nature of the resurrection body, but he states that it is different from the physical body with which we live during our normal lifetimes. Paul says that bodies of fish are different from the bodies of birds. The moon is different from the stars. "The splendor of the heavenly bodies is one kind, and the splendor of the earthly bodies is another" (v. 40). Resurrection bodies will be different from physical bodies because they will be "spiritual" (v. 44).

Comparison with the stories of Jesus' appearances after His resurrection suggests some of the similarities and some of the differences. The resurrection body will be similar to the physical body in that we will be recognizable. It will have form and substance. The resurrection body will be able to speak, see, touch, and be touched. On the other hand, Jesus apparently was able to move through walls or doors in His resurrected body. He was able to disappear almost instantly. The substance will not be identical to our present physical substance.

Comparison to Jesus' brief resurrection appearances does not answer all our questions about the kind of body the resurrection body will be. However, the differences and similarities have important implications for us. Many people have worried that cremation would make resurrection impossible. Such a worry is unfounded. It fails to recognize that the resurrected body is spiritual, not physical. Paul promises in Philippians 3:21 that God "will transform the body of our humiliation into conformity with his glorified body" (author's translation). God is able to construct the physical body from whatever physical remains are left. We expect people who have lost limbs to be resurrected whole. Though Scripture is not explicit, the analogy of Christ would suggest that no matter what deformities and congenital birth defects exist in the physical body, the resurrection body will be whole.

That transformation is the miracle of the resurrection. Such faith goes beyond physics and medical science. Resurrection is the work of God, not the product of nature.

The Importance of Resurrection Faith

Some people suggest that the idea of resurrection was a primitive, Jewish notion that belongs to ancient culture. They imply that modern, sophisticated Christians do not need to believe in the resurrection of Jesus nor look forward to a future resurrection of the dead. The irony of such an argument is that it was first raised against the Christian hope of resurrection less than 25 years after Jesus' resurrection. In 1 Corinthians 15 (written about A.D. 53) Paul addresses the problem of people who didn't believe in resurrection. The apostle contends that faith in the Resurrection is absolutely central to being a Christian. For no other doctrine does Paul insist that Christian faith rises or falls upon its truth. Yet he does for resurrection. Verses 12-19 show that the Christian faith is a hoax unless Christ was raised from the dead and a future resurrection will happen. In a real sense, faith in the resurrection of Christ and the hope of our resurrection are the factors that distinguish Christianity from any other religious hope.

Paul also saw the resurrection of Christ as the basis of holy living. In Romans 6 and Colossians 3 he speaks of being united with Christ in His death by means of our baptism. Union with Christ's death brings our salvation. Since we are united with Christ in His death, we are also united with Him in His resurrection. Paul says that union with Christ in resurrection means that we can live a new quality of life in the present time. Since death resulted from sin (Romans 5:12-14 and 6:23), Christ's victory over death meant that the power of sin had also been broken. Thus, the Christian life is to be one of victory over the power of sin.

Do We Have to Die to Be Raised from the Dead?

The centrality of the resurrection for Christians raises another interesting question. In relation to the Second Coming, what happens to the bodies of people who are alive at that point in time? Do we have to die to experience the resurrection? Believers in the Church raised that same question at Thessalonica as early as A.D. 51. Responding to them in 1 Thessalonians 4:16-17, Paul wrote, "For the Lord himself will come down from heaven, . . . and the dead in Christ will rise first. After that, we who are still alive . . . will be caught up together with them in the clouds to meet the Lord in the air. And so we will be with the Lord forever."

The word that describes living Christians being caught up to meet Christ is "rapture." The Rapture takes place immediately after the resurrection of believers as part of the whole event of Christ's second coming. Paul does not envision it as a frightening time. The next verse reads, "Therefore encourage each other with these words" (v. 18). The Rapture is the time and way living Christians will have their physical bodies transformed into resurrection bodies without going through death.

What About Nonbelievers?

It is interesting that all of Paul's discussion of resurrection is about the resurrection of believers. None of his letters deals with the question of whether or not the wicked are raised. However, other parts of the Bible speak to this question. Acts quotes a speech of Paul in which the apostle states, "There will be a resurrection of both the righteous and the wicked" (24:15). In John 5:28-29, Jesus declares, "The hour is coming when all those in the tombs will hear His voice and will come out; those who have done good things for the resurrection of life, and those who have done evil things for the resurrection of judgment" (author's translation).

The question of whether the resurrection of the righteous for their reward and the resurrection of the wicked for judgment will happen at the same time or one after another is debated. One would probably assume from Acts 24:15 and John 5:28-29 that both righteous and wicked will be raised at the same time and then their fates announced. However, Revelation 20:5 speaks of "the first resurrection." Followers of dispensationalism and historic premillennialism believe that this implies a second resurrection. The first resurrection would be of the righteous and would take place before the millennium. The second resurrection would involve the wicked and would occur after the millennium. Verses 13-15 speak of the sea, death, and Hades giving up their dead so they could be judged. Revelation does not call this a second resurrection, but many Bible scholars do. The Bible is not clear about how or when the resurrection of the wicked will take place. Scripture was not written to answer such questions. It was written to prepare believers for the hope God has prepared for us.

Conclusion

The New Testament clearly understands the resurrection as the great hope of the Christian faith. Christians who have come to genuinely understand and believe in the resurrection face death very differently than do unbelievers. However, funerals and times of personal grief are not the times to teach these truths. They need to be taught on a regular basis to all of God's people. Then, at the time of death and grief we can celebrate our hope of resurrection.

Background Scripture: Luke 20:27; John 5:28-29; Acts 4:1-2; 23:6-9; 24:15; Romans 5:12-14; 6; 1 Corinthians 15; Philippians 3:21; Colossians 3; 1 Thessalonians 4:16-18; Revelation 20:5, 13-15

IMPORTANT WORDS IN THIS CHAPTER

See *Glossary* for definitions.

Covenant

Gentiles

CHAPTER 12

"... But After This the Judgment"

ONE OF THE FIRST COMPLETE SENTENCES A YOUNG child will construct is, "That's not fair!" From a very early age human beings have a strong sense of justice, though it is usually expressed as a strong objection to suffering injustice.

That sense of demanding what is fair never leaves a human being. C. S. Lewis noticed the fact that human beings of all ages and all cultures share such a feeling. He said that its existence is evidence for the existence of God. Only God could have placed such a perception in people. Evolutionary theory cannot adequately explain it. The strong sense of justice in small children bears witness to a God who has placed justice in the fabric of the reality of the universe.

The Christian doctrine of the final Judgment is not a device of theologians to create fear in people's hearts. Rather, it is the acknowledgment that the God who created us and the world cannot and will not tolerate unfairness forever. What is right must be recognized and rewarded. What is wrong must be pointed out and punished. Anything less is "not fair."

Old Testament Foundations

The biblical idea of judgment begins in the Old Testament. It is part of the fabric of covenant relationship with God. The covenant that God made with Israel promised them rewards for obedience and punishment for disobedience (Deuteronomy 27—28). We clearly see the influence of this theology in 2 Kings 17. The author boldly declared that the national catastrophes falling on Israel were a result of the nation's sins.

As the prophets preached, they became aware that some in Israel were obedient, while others were disobedient. Isaiah spoke of a remnant that would cause God to keep His promises of saving and preserving Israel. Lest the wicked think that their sins would remain unpunished forever, the prophets began to speak of the "day of the Lord." The "day of the Lord" would be at the end of time, when sin would be punished and righteousness rewarded. Isaiah, Amos, and Joel especially saw the "day of the Lord" as a time of judgment.

During the centuries between the Old and New Testaments, Judaism became much more specific in its understanding of God's judgment. With the appearance of a theology of resurrection, nonbiblical writers saw the time of judgment happening after the resurrection. The eternal destiny of both the righteous and the wicked was to be determined by the Judgment. Writers in the period between the Old and New Testaments usually described God as the Judge, but some believed the Messiah would carry out that role.

New Testament Teachings

The clearest teaching about the Judgment comes in the New Testament. The Old Testament idea that judgment happens in the present still appears. In John 3:17-21 Jesus taught that judgment is a present reality, not just a future idea. Romans 1:18 speaks of "the wrath of God . . . being revealed" (present tense) against every kind of sin and wickedness.

However, the main thrust of New Testament passages about the Judgment is as a future event. At the end of time the Judgment will take place. Romans 2:2-3 speaks of the judgment of God. Verse 5 begins to reveal the details of this

Judgment. "Because of your stubbornness and your unrepentant heart, you are storing up wrath against yourself for the day of God's wrath, when his righteous judgment will be revealed." When that day comes, God "will give to each person according to what he has done" (v. 6). Eternal life will be the reward of those whose good works show that they patiently "seek glory, honor and immortality" (v. 7). On the other hand, wrath, distress, and tribulation will be reserved for those who do not obey the truth. Paul clearly sees a day coming when everyone will be judged according to the life he or she has lived.

Second Corinthians 5:10 also speaks of a coming day of judgment. Paul writes, "For we must all appear before the judgment seat of Christ, that each one may receive what is due him for the things done while in the body, whether good or bad." By using the term "judgment seat," the apostle was drawing on a familiar picture in Corinth. At the end of the main street of the city was the judgment seat, a high platform where the city ruler sat to hear legal cases. Justice in the form of punishment for evil and reward for good was meted out there. In the same way Paul portrays Christ as the Judge in the Corinthian passage.

Second Thessalonians 1:5-10 associates God's judgment with the second coming of Christ. Paul states that the suffering the Thessalonians were enduring was evidence of "the righteous judgment of God" (KJV). In the future God would send affliction on the ones afflicting them. The Lord would also send relief to the distressed Thessalonians. Verse 7 indicates that this righteous judgment would take place "at the revelation of the Lord Jesus from heaven with His mighty angels" (author's translation). Eternal punishment will be meted out to those who "do not obey the gospel" when "he comes to be glorified" (vv. 8-10). The exact timing of judgment in relationship to resurrection and rapture is not specified. However, the Judgment will clearly take place in connection with the Second Coming.

The final judgment scene described in the New Testament appears in Revelation 20:11-15. This is often referred to as the Great White Throne Judgment because verse 11 mentions "a great white throne." Here the books that contain the records of everyone's life are opened, and the dead are judged according to what they have done in life. The dead come from the sea, death, and Hades (the place of the dead) to be judged. This is a word picture teaching that no one will avoid this final Judgment. No matter the manner of death or where one's body is buried, everyone will make an appearance at the final Judgment.

The New Testament teaching is clear: Everyone will be judged. Judgment is part of the chain of events associated with the Second Coming. Judgment will be based on one's works.

What Will Be Decided at the Judgment?

Many people think of the Judgment as the time when God decides who will be saved and who will be eternally lost. While that may be an issue at the Judgment, most of the biblical references are not concerned about that question. In the minds of biblical authors that question is already decided. John 3:18 states, "Whoever believes in him is not condemned, but whoever does not believe stands condemned already because he has not believed in the name of God's one and only Son." The Judgment may reveal those who will be saved and those who will be lost, but it does not determine that. That decision is being made every moment by the choices people make in this life.

The parable of the talents found in Matthew 25:14-30 suggests that the Judgment will reveal who is lost and who is saved as well as apportion the rewards for those who are saved. The servants who received five talents and two talents are contrasted with the servant who was given one talent. The day of accounting led to the condemnation of the one servant who failed to obey his master's instructions. For the two obedient servants the day of reckoning brought more than "salvation." Both were rewarded in proportion to their work.

Most New Testament passages tend to present the Judgment as the time when the rewards for righteousness and the punishments for evil are revealed. Several passages mentioned above speak of judgment according to a person's works. If the purpose of judgment was to determine whether or not a person was saved, salvation would be by works. The New Testament clearly teaches that people are saved by grace through faith, not by works (Romans 3:20; Galatians 3:10-14; and Ephesians 2:8-9). Since the Judgment will deal with works, its purpose is to identify the reward or punishment that will be received.

First Corinthians 3:10-17 is instructive at this point, though not easy to understand. Paul was describing the judgment of the works of Christian leaders. Everything was built on the common foundation of Jesus Christ. Yet the varying ways in which different leaders conducted their ministry were contrasting manners of building on Christ, the Foundation. Some forms of ministry produced valuable results—"gold, silver, [or] precious stones." Other methods of ministering produced less enduring results—"wood, hay, [and] stubble" (v. 12, KJV). The fires of judgment would reveal the quality of each leader's work.

Paul was using figurative language in the whole paragraph, but he clearly states that the salvation of the individual leaders was not at stake. All of them will be saved, though some will be saved through the fire of judgment. The judgment process will evaluate the works of each leader. The rewards will be proportionate to the quality of ministry that leader gave.

Judgment will apportion the rewards of the righteous to each one according to his or her good works. Judgment will also assign the punishment earned by the unrighteous. Revelation 20:10 speaks of a lake of fire and sulfur. Anyone whose name is not written in the book of life will be thrown into the lake of fire (v. 15). Verse 14 states that death and Hades will also be thrown into this lake of fire. This word picture communicates torment. The Judgment will mark the end of opportunity for the wicked. All that remains is the torment of being eternally cut off from the presence of God while knowing one could have enjoyed His presence forever.

In addition to "fire," New Testament writers use words like "darkness" (Matthew 25:30), "wrath" (Romans 2:5), "everlasting destruction" (2 Thessalonians 1:9), and "second death" (Revelation 20:14) to describe the fate of those who refuse to be saved. The variety of words shows that the authors of the New Testament were trying to express a reality too horrible for words. The real reward for the righteous is to always be with the Lord (1 Thessalonians 4:17). The real punishment for the wicked is eternal separation from the God who alone brings meaning and fulfillment to the human heart.

Will God's Judgment Be Fair?

Unfortunately many human beings are deeply suspicious of God. Most will not directly accuse Him of incompetence because the very suggestion sounds so blasphemous. However, the "what about . . . ?" questions reveal the suspicion of many that He will not be fair. The questions themselves may be genuine, but they reveal a frightening lack of knowledge of God.

"What about those who have never heard the gospel?" This question is a product of the burden of compassionate Christians that those who do not know Christ personally will be lost. Romans 1—2 makes it clear that God will judge people fairly on the basis of what they do know. Romans 2:12 states that those who have the law (Jews) will be judged on the basis of the law. Those who do not have the law, but sinned against what God had made known to them, will be judged without reference to the law. Verses 14-16 describe

Gentiles who have never heard of the law or the gospel. However, what they need to know is "written on their hearts" (v. 15), according to Paul. God will judge the "secret [thoughts]" (v. 16) of all. That is, everyone will be judged on the basis of what they knew and how they responded to that light they had.

"What about infants who die before they understand the gospel?" Romans 2 still applies. They will be judged on the basis of what they knew. If they understood nothing, they will not be held accountable by God. Mentally impaired people will be judged on the basis of their understanding. Paul's conclusion is clearly stated in verse 2: "God's judgment . . . is based on truth." His judgment is reliable. Only human arrogance questions His ability to judge rightly.

Won't Everybody Be Saved Eventually?

The question of whether the judgment of God is final or remedial has always been raised. Does God's pronouncement of judgment banish sinners forever, or can it somehow rescue and restore them? There are two reasons why people ask this question. First, it is difficult for some people to reconcile the idea of a loving God with a final and eternal condemnation of the wicked. This point can be refined and presented in several ways. However, the bottom line of this view is that the nature and purpose of God are inconsistent with eternal condemnation. Second, the apostle Paul speaks in some places in a way that seems to suggest that ultimately everyone will be saved.

In Colossians 1:20 Paul speaks of Christ reconciling all things to himself. If "all things" is taken literally, it would mean that everyone would be saved in the end. It also would mean the ultimate salvation of Satan and the demonic world. Philippians 2:9-11 talks about every knee bowing and every tongue confessing the Lordship of Christ. However, universal acknowledgment of Christ is not the same as universal salvation. The end of time may bring the end of rebellion against God, but eternal punishment for a life of rebellion will be meted out (2 Thessalonians 1:9-10).

The objection that God's nature and purpose are incompatible with eternal judgment cannot be answered with an isolated text. Every text about judgment can be met with a text about love. The philosophical question finally turns on this: could God, even a God of love, who is also holy and just, leave sin forever unpunished? From youngest child to wisest theologian, most people answer, "That wouldn't be fair."

Conclusion

The Bible does not answer every philosophical question we can ask about the punishment of the lost. Such information is not necessary for believers. We have been assured that salvation is by grace through faith. Our names can be written in the book of life. All that the Judgment will do for us is evaluate the faithfulness of our obedience. "Well done, good and faithful servant!" (Matthew 25:21, 23) is the announcement awaiting all who "walk in the light, as he is in the light" (1 John 1:7).

Background Scripture: Deuteronomy 27—28; 2 Kings 17; Matthew 25:14-30; John 3:17-21; Romans 1—2; 3:20; 1 Corinthians 3:10-17; 2 Corinthians 5:10; Galatians 3:10-14; Ephesians 2:8-9; Philippians 2:9-11; Colossians 1:20; 1 Thessalonians 4:17; 2 Thessalonians 1:5-10; 1 John 1:7; Revelation 20:10-15

SECTION IV

Conclusion

by David Kendall

David Kendall, Ph.D., is senior pastor of
the McPherson Free Methodist Church,
McPherson, Kansas.

Important Words in This Chapter

See *Glossary* for definitions.

Anticipation

Joy

Opportunity

Trust

CHAPTER 13

What Now?

"TIME!" WHEN THE TEACHER SAID IT, THE TEST WAS over. Often, however, I was not finished. Hearing that abrupt word made me panic. First, I regretted past hours when I did not study. Then I feared the consequences. Knowing that this was the end did not make me happy.

As Christians, we have a much different view of the end. Hearing God shout "time!" will not fill us with panic or fear. Rather, we will finally be all He calls us to be. We will finally receive all He promises us. Finally, we will experience fully His kingdom. As Christians we eagerly wait for God to shout "time!"

The End Is Now

In one way God has already shouted "time!" That is, the end has begun. The end is now.

Of course, Jesus has not yet returned. For all we know, our world and our lives will go on for years. Obviously, if we are counting hours and days, the end is not now.

Nevertheless, think about what God promises to do at the end. If we think about the meaning and purpose of Christian life, the end *is* now.

That is because Jesus has come. Through His life, death, and resurrection, God's plan for the world and for us are as good as accomplished. Jesus broke into history to speak and act for God. Jesus' story is familiar to us. His coming shows

119

us who God is and what God wants. In response to Jesus, we humans wanted our own way. As a result, He was crucified. Although that seemed like the end of Jesus, God raised Him from the dead. Now anyone who trusts Jesus becomes a new creation (2 Corinthians 5:17).

In other words, Jesus' coming brings history to its proper end. His death and resurrection signal the beginning of "a new heaven and a new earth" (2 Peter 3:13; Revelation 21:1; see 2 Corinthians 5:17). When we trust Jesus as Savior and Lord, we share in the new thing God is doing. For us the end times have come. Indeed, the end is now.

By definition, then, Christian life is end-time life. A new and final age began with the coming of Jesus. We could call it the original and true "new age"! Jesus ushers in the "last days" (see Hebrews 1:1-2) when this present world passes away (see 1 Corinthians 7:31) and God sets up His kingdom once for all. Certainly we must wait for the Kingdom to come fully. Even so, we are privileged to experience a Kingdom life right now. Already we experience end time reality.

Let me give several examples of this. One day we will stand before God, and He will declare us pardoned because we have trusted Jesus. Yet, "there is now no condemnation for those who are in Christ Jesus" (Romans 8:1). On the final day we will be like Christ (1 John 3:2). Already, however, "we . . . are being transformed into his likeness with ever-increasing glory" (2 Corinthians 3:18). In heaven we will enjoy intimate and wonderful fellowship with Christ himself (Philippians 1:23; 2 Corinthians 5:6-8).

Right now, however, as we are in Christ, God's Spirit gives us intimacy with God as Father. We cry "Abba," or "dear," Father (Galatians 4:6). When God's kingdom comes fully, He will bring complete restoration of all things. He will make right everything that has gone wrong in the world and human life (Romans 8:18-25). Yet, meanwhile, God works to restore us in miraculous ways. Often in the Body of Christ, through the prayers of God's people, healing comes to us. In all these ways, and others, "the powers of the coming age" (Hebrews 6:5) already work in our world and lives. For us the end is now.

The apostle Paul drew a word picture to help us understand this truth. He called Jesus the "firstfruits" of the new creation (see Paul's discussion in 1 Corinthians 15). After farmers plant their crops, they must wait. They prepare their fields, plant the seeds, water generously, and then they wait. As time passes, they look for signs of the coming harvest. When they finally see the firstfruits, they know the harvest is on the way. Jesus is like the "firstfruits." What happened to Him signals what is happening to all His followers.

Of course, for the farmer who has seen the firstfruits, there comes an actual moment we would call "the end," that is, the harvest. Similarly, at some future moment God will shout "time!" Then God will finish what He has already begun to do in our world and lives. Our experience of His love and power now makes us long for more. We are eager to hear God call "time!"

What We Know for Sure

What can we say about this moment when God will shout "time!" At least five things. To begin, we *do* know that this moment will come. Jesus *will* return to bring history to a fitting end. How do we know? First, Jesus promised He would return (Matthew 24:30; 26:64). Both the Bible and our experience tell us that He does whatever He promises. Second, when Jesus ascended to heaven, His disciples received assurance of His return (Acts 1:11). Third, the resurrection of Jesus from the dead assures us. His resurrection points us to a future time when God will raise us. The New Testament identifies our resurrection with the return of Christ in power (see 1 Thessalonians 4:16 and 1 Corinthians 15:20-24).

Here's a second thing we can say. Although Christ will come, we do not know when. Jesus himself said, "No one knows about that day or hour, not even the angels in heaven, nor the Son, but only the Father" (Mark 13:32). Certainly the

New Testament lists signs of the end of the age (see Matthew 24; Mark 13; and Luke 21). These passages have led some to do what Jesus said cannot be done. They have tried to figure when He will come. Doing this is not wise. Jesus tells us about these signs so that we will always be ready for His return. Most of the signs are various forms of evil or trouble that often appear in history. To be sure, they will appear one final time (like Jesus). The point is, however, that *whenever* these troubles occur, we must be ready!

Third, whether the time comes sooner or later, we can trust God. He created time and keeps time running. At some moment He will end time. God is never early, nor is He late. He is always on time. With time, as with everything else, God remains trustworthy.

Fourth, we know what God does with the time on His hands. For Him, time is opportunity. Peter wrote, "The Lord is not slow in keeping his promise, as some understand slowness. He is patient with you, not wanting anyone to perish, but everyone to come to repentance" (2 Peter 3:9). The more time there is, the more opportunity for people to know Jesus. Not one second passes without God desiring and working to save lost people.

Finally, we know that God reaches people through us. As long as there *is* time, God gives us a great honor. He makes us His representatives who witness to His saving work. God uses us to offer end time or eternal life to all—now.

What Now?

As Jesus' followers, we live in the light of that future moment when God will shout "time!" That moment should make a tremendous difference in our everyday lives. Let me suggest several ways.

Don't worry about the timing of Jesus' return. Some people become too excited about the latest development in the Middle East. They draw charts, coordinate calendars, and synchronize watches. Resist the temptation.

Actually, when we consider what God does with us and around us every day, we will become excited. Our spiritual adrenaline will pump no matter what is happening on the other side of the world. That's because, as we've seen, the end *is* now. Every day and every moment has eternal significance. The psalmist asks the Lord, "Teach us to number our days aright, that we may gain a heart of wisdom" (90:12). As followers of Jesus, we have even more reason to appreciate and make the most of every day.

As believers we can embrace fully and deeply the life God offers us. We should drink deeply of the living waters of God's Spirit (John 7:37-39). We may offer ourselves enthusiastically to God as a living sacrifice (Romans 12:1). God's grace will keep us from following the ways of this world, which are passing away. God's Spirit will continually renew our inner life (v. 2).

Remember: Jesus determines our destiny. As He is, so we are and will be. As He goes, so we go. Therefore, we pursue Christlike qualities of character and conduct. We seek to *be* like Jesus and to *act* like Jesus. Above all, we need to be filled with Christ's love—for God and for others.

Since Jesus determines our destiny, we should fill whatever time we have with the things He would do. We must be about the Master's business. Time, talents, and energy become tools for His work. No matter how it seems at any given moment, we are confident that Jesus is at work. Within us and through us He works to accomplish God's saving plans in the world.

Finally, we can anticipate and rejoice, no matter the time and the circumstances. We are on the winning side! As we trust Jesus, all that we recognize now as good will be better when He returns (perhaps soon!). He will remove all that seems bad now. In this way, whether facing good or bad, we have a reason to celebrate. In the end—which *has* already begun—Christ will have His way. Thus, already we have cause to rejoice "with an inexpressible and glorious joy" (1 Peter 1:8).

When God shouts "time!" there will be nothing left to complete. God will have brought all things to a proper conclusion. Believers in Jesus will have no regrets over the past and no fear of the future. In the end we will be very happy and fulfill what we were created to do—to glorify God eternally. Because that is so, let the celebration begin now!

Not the End—the Beginning

Background Scripture: Psalm 90:12; Matthew 24; 26:64; Mark 13; Luke 21; John 7:37-39; Acts 1:11; Romans 8:1, 18-25; 12:1-2; 1 Corinthians 7:31; 15:1-58; 2 Corinthians 3:18; 5:6-8, 17; Galatians 4:6; Philippians 1:23; 1 Thessalonians 4:16; Hebrews 1:1-2; 6:5; 1 Peter 1:8; 2 Peter 3:9, 11-13; 1 John 3:2-3; Revelation 21:1

APPENDIX 1

Articles of Faith

The Free Methodist Church: **XVIII. The Return of Christ**

Λ/127. The return of Christ is certain and may occur at any moment, although it is not given us to know the hour. At His return He will fulfill all prophecies concerning His final triumph over all evil. The believer's response is joyous expectation, watchfulness, readiness, and diligence.

The Constitution of The Free Methodist Church (Indianapolis: Light and Life Press, 1989), 15.

The Church of the Nazarene: **XV. Second Coming of Christ**

19. We believe that the Lord Jesus Christ will come again; that we who are alive at His coming shall not precede them that are asleep in Christ Jesus; but that, if we are abiding in Him, we shall be caught up with the risen saints to meet the Lord in the air, so that we shall ever be with the Lord.

Manual/1993-97 Church of the Nazarene (Kansas City: Nazarene Publishing House, 1993), 33.

The Wesleyan Church: **XVIII. The Second Coming of Christ**

244. We believe that the certainty of the personal and imminent return of Christ inspires holy living and zeal for the evangelization of the world. At His return He will fulfill all prophecies made concerning His final and complete triumph over evil.

The Discipline of The Wesleyan Church (Indianapolis: Wesleyan Publishing House, 1992), 27.

APPENDIX 2

Comparison of End Time Views

	Premillennial	Postmillennial	Amillennial
Bible Interpretation	Literal	Symbolic	Spiritual (or Allegorical)
Israel	Church and Israel are separate. Church has not taken over promises to Israel. Literal fulfillment of promises to Israel (even a remnant) important before the end will come.	Israel and Church equal one people of God. Israel only important as symbol.	No future for Israel. Church took over promises because Israel failed to meet the conditions of God.
1,000-Year Reign	Literal Kingdom on earth after Tribulation and Second Coming	Spiritual 1,000 years of peace before Second Coming	None (or is a present reality)
Rapture Timing	5 choices: Pretribulation, midtribulation, prewrath, partial at 5¼ years into tribulation, posttribulation	None	Coincides with Second Coming
Tribulation Effect on Church	Pretribulation: Church in heaven during Tribulation Midtribulation: Church in heaven last 3½ years of Tribulation Prewrath: Church in heaven during"wrath" (last 1¼ years of Tribulation). Partial: Spiritual Church in heaven during Tribulation; rest of Church tested. Posttribulation: Church endures 7-year Tribulation	None	None. All saints, living and dead, will be raptured.

Worldview	Expect increased apostasy. History is divided into ages (dispensations) in which God works in differing ways.	Preaching the gospel will Christianize the world. Kingdom is now present and growing.	Promise of salvation through Christ is most important aspect. World's conditions worsen approaching Second Coming.
Resurrection	Two: Saints at Rapture, sinners after 1,000-year reign	One: Of all people, at Second Coming	One: Of all people, at Second Coming
Judgment	Of sinners, after 1,000-year reign	Of everyone, at Second Coming	Of everyone, at Second Coming
Heaven/Hell	Literal, after 1,000-year reign	Fullness begins after Second Coming.	Eternity follows the Second Coming.

GLOSSARY

Abomination (uh-BAHM-uh-NAY-shun) **of desolation**: Something that causes extreme disgust and hatred. Any idol was an abomination to God. If someone placed an idol in the Temple, that made the Temple unclean. The Temple had to be cleansed before the people could worship there again. This term is found in Matthew 24:15, KJV, Mark 13:14, KJV. (Similar wording is found in Daniel 8:13; 9:27; 11:31; 12:11.)

Amillennialism (AH-mi-LEN-ee-ul-IZ-um): The belief that the millennium is the present reign of Christ in the Church. The 1,000 years is not literal but is a symbol that Christ is already reigning. He is already bringing peace on earth through the Church.

Antiochus (an-TIE-a-cus) **IV**: King of Syria from 175 to 163 B.C. In 167 B.C. he attacked Jerusalem and desecrated the Temple.

Anti-Semitism (AN-tee-SE-muh-ti-zum): Hostility toward or discrimination against Jews.

Apocalypse (uh-PAHK-uh-lips): A Greek word that means "revelation." An apocalypse is a special kind of Jewish or Christian writing that says God will destroy evil and set up His kingdom. Apocalypses contain accounts of visions and images that are difficult for modern readers to understand.

Apocalyptic (uh-PAHK-uh-LIP-tik): An adjective that describes special kinds of Jewish and Christian writings and religious beliefs that are similar to the Book of Revelation.

Armageddon (AHR-muh-GED-un): The name of a large valley in northern Israel. The Bible usually calls this valley Jezreel. The valley is located near the mountain of Megiddo. In Hebrew, Armageddon means "mountain of Megiddo." Armageddon is considered to be the site of the final battle between God and evil. (See Revelation 16:16.)

Buddhism (BEW-diz-um): A religion that arose in India in the 500s B.C. The founder of Buddhism was Gautama Buddha. Gautama was his family name. Buddha means "the Enlightened One." He thought he found the true meaning of life, and the Buddha taught how to be free from suffering in his "Four Noble Truths."

Calvinism (KAL-vun-iz-um): Theology based on the teachings of John Calvin (1509-64). Calvinism differs from Wesleyanism in many important ways—notably that only those predestined by God can be saved, and once chosen they cannot lose their salvation.

Completed (also called "preterist") **apocalyptic**: A view that holds that all apocalyptic writings were understandable only in the time and circumstances of the original readers.

Covenant (KUV-uh-nunt): A bond entered into voluntarily by two parties by which each pledges to do something for the other. The idea of covenant between God and the people of Israel is basic to the religion of the Old Testament.

Cyclical (SICK-le-kul) **time**: Time seen as a series of events that recur regularly and lead back to the starting point. These cycles are seen as endless repetitions.

Cyclical Time

Dead Sea Scrolls: A group of ancient writings found in caves near Qumran by the Dead Sea in 1947. They include the oldest copies of the Old Testament and writing by Jews who lived there shortly before the time of Jesus.

Dispensation (DIS-pun-SAY-shun): A plan for doing something, and the way the plan is carried out. Christian doctrine uses the word in a special way. It refers to the ways God has carried out His plan for the world.

Dispensational premillennialism (DIS-pun-SAY-shun-ul PREE-muh-LEN-ee-ul-IZ-um): The belief in dispensational views and that Christ will return *before* the millennium. Dispensationalists believe that human beings are saved in different ways in the separate periods (or dispensations) of history, that all the promises of the Old Testament to Israel will be literally fulfilled during the millennium, and that at the end of the millennium the judgment of unbelievers will take place. This view is also known for its special teaching about the secret Rapture of the Church, although proponents differ whether it will occur before, during, or after a seven-year period of tribulation. Most of the popular writers who promote dispensational premillennialism come from the Calvinist and Reformed theological traditions.

Dispensationalism (DIS-pun-SAY-shun-ul-iz-um): The teaching that God acts in different ways at different times in history. Its proponents usually divide history into seven periods (or dispensations).

Domitian (doe-MI-shun): Emperor of Rome from A.D. 81 to 96. He demanded that public worship be given to him as *Dominus et Deus* (Lord and God). A persecution of Jews and Christians broke out near the end of his reign. The apostle John received his visions recorded in the Book of Revelation during this persecution.

Eschatology (ES-kuh-TAH-luh-jee): The doctrine about the end of the world or last times. The word comes from two Greek words that mean "the study of last things."

Existentialism (egg-zis-TEN-sha-li-zum): A chiefly 20th-century philosophical movement embracing diverse doctrines but centering on analysis of individual existence in an unfathomable universe. It also focuses on the plight of the individual who must assume ultimate responsibility for his or her acts of free will without any certain knowledge of what is right or wrong or good or bad.

Figurative language: Symbolic language. Language that intentionally deviates from the ordinary meaning or form to indicate another level of meaning.

Futurist apocalyptic (FYEW-che-rist uh-PAHK-uh-LIP-tik): This view sees apocalyptic literature as a prediction of the end of time only in the future. The material had no meaning for those who lived when it was written.

Futuristic eschatology (fyew-che-RIS-tik ES-kuh-TAH-luh-jee): The idea that the kingdom of God is yet to come in the future and does not exist presently.

Gaius (GAY-us) (also known as Caligula): Roman emperor who lived from A.D. 12 to 41 and reigned from A.D. 37 to 41.

Gehenna (ga-HEN-uh): The name of the place where trash from Jerusalem was burned. The New Testament also uses this Greek word for hell.

Gentiles (JEN-tiles): Persons who are not Jews. The Hebrew and Greek words for Gentile mean "people" or "nations." The Jews called all nations other than their own "Gentile."

Gog (GAHG): In Revelation 20:8, Gog and Magog are two powers under the dominion of Satan. In the Old Testament they are mentioned together in Ezekiel 38:2 where, however, Gog is a people (apparently the Scythians who ravaged western Asia about 630 B.C.) and Magog a land. In apocalyptic literature Gog is a figure for those opposed to the people of God.

Hades (HAY-deez): The place the New Testament says people go after death. *Hadēs* is the Greek word for "grave." Sometimes *Hadēs* is translated "hell."

Heresy (HAIR-uh-see): A false belief or practice that departs from Christian truth.

Heretical (he-RE-ti-kal): An adjective used to describe a false belief or practice.

Hinduism (HIN-dew-iz-um): A religion that began in India about 3,500 years ago. No one person started Hinduism. There are so many forms of it that Hinduism is really a family of religions. Hindus believe that the world does not have lasting value. They also believe there are many ways to find salvation.

Historic premillennialism (hi-STOR-ik PREE-muh-LEN-ee-ul-IZ-um): The belief that Christ will return *before* the 1,000 years of peace. This view does not contain the concept of dispensations (see dispensational premillennialism).

Historical apocalyptic (hi-STOR-i-kal uh-PAHK-uh-LIP-tik): This view sees apocalyptic literature as the history of the Church from beginning to end written in advance.

Immanence (IM-uh-nuns): A word meaning that God is present in the world. God is related to the world in a close way. The world exists because God exists in it.

Inaugurated eschatology (i-NAW-gyuh-rayt-ed ES-kuh-TAH-luh-jee): The idea that Jesus brought the Kingdom as part of His ministry, but the Kingdom will not be complete until obedience to God becomes universal and the Kingdom becomes eternal.

Linear (LI-nee-ur) **time**: The way of viewing time as having a starting point and an ending point. The future is not a repetition of the past.

Linear Time

Marxism (MARK-si-zum): The political, economic, and social principles advocated by Karl Marx. Sometimes popularly referred to as "communism" or "socialism."

Materialism (ma-TEER-ee-uh-li-zum): The belief that possessions are more important than anything else. Materialism places higher value on money and property than on the kingdom of God.

Messiah (muh-SIE-uh): A person chosen by God to do His will. The word "Messiah" in Hebrew means "the Anointed One." The Jews hoped for a future king from the family of David to be their Messiah. "Christ" is the Greek word for Messiah. Christians believe that Jesus was the Messiah.

Messianic (MES-ee-AN-ik): An adjective used to describe a person or thing that is related to the promised Messiah.

Millennium (mi-LEN-ee-um): A term derived from the Latin expression for 1,000 years. It refers to the 1,000-year reign of Christ, which will be a time of peace on earth.

Near-death experience: A vision of the afterlife that some people claim to have when they come close to dying.

Nero (NEE-roh): A Roman who lived from A.D. 37 to 68 and was emperor from A.D. 54. He is best known as the emperor responsible for much of the destruction when Rome burned in A.D. 64.

Nihilism (NIEH-uh-li-zum): A viewpoint that traditional beliefs and values are unfounded and that existence is useless and meaningless.

Omnipresence (ahm-ni-PREZ-uns): The quality of God that means He is everywhere. His presence is limited by neither time nor space.

Omniscience (ahm-NISH-uns): The attribute of God that means He knows all that can be known.

Postmillennialism (POHST-muh-LEN-ee-ul-IZ-um): The belief that Christ will return *after* the millennium, or 1,000-year reign of peace. This belief includes the idea that the millennium will be brought in by a large part of humanity accepting Christ as the result of hearing the gospel preached.

Premillennialism (PREE-muh-LEN-ee-ul-IZ-um): The belief that Christ will return *before* the millennium, or 1,000-year reign of peace. This is a part of the belief of both historic premillennialism and dispensational premillennialism.

Prophecy (PRAHF-uh-see): A divinely inspired message from God to people. The message can urge people to repent and obey God, tell of judgment that God will send, or predict future events.

Rapture (RAP-cher): The term used to describe what will happen to living believers when Christ comes again. They will be "caught up . . . to meet the Lord" (1 Thessalonians 4:17). Some say the Rapture will occur at the Second Coming. They are two parts of the same event. Dispensationalism says that the Rapture is the secret return of Christ before the Great Tribulation. The Second Coming will occur seven years later.

Rationalist (RASH-nuh-list): One who is reliant on reason or logic as the basis for establishment of religious truth.

Realized eschatology (REE-uh-lized ES-kuh-TAH-luh-jee): The idea that the kingdom of God is a present reality rather than a future event.

Reincarnation (ree-in-kar-NAY-shun): The belief that souls migrate at death from one body into another until complete purification is achieved. This belief is fundamentally at odds with the Christian doctrine of the resurrection of the body.

Resurrection (REZ-uh-REK-shun): The belief that those who have died will return to life in a bodily form at the second coming of Christ.

Resuscitation (re-suh-suh-TAY-shun): To revive from apparent death or from unconsciousness.

Second Coming: The term used to refer to the return of Jesus Christ to earth.

Sheol (SHEE-ohl): The Hebrew word for the region to which the dead go. Sometimes *Sheol* refers to the sorrows of death, but it usually means the place where the dead wait for the resurrection. *Sheol* does not mean the same as hell or Gehenna.

Symbolic apocalyptic (sim-BAH-lik uh-PAHK-uh-LIP-tik): This view sees the symbolism of apocalyptic literature as designed to express universal and abstract theological truths, ignoring the specific circumstances when the material was written.

Synagogue (SIN-uh-GAHG): A place of worship for Jews. A synagogue can be organized wherever 10 or more males meet for worship.

Synoptic (si-NAHP-tik): An adjective used to describe material that shares a common view. The word comes from two Greek words meaning "seen together." Matthew, Mark, and Luke are called the Synoptic Gospels because their words and order of events about Jesus' life are very much alike.

Theism (THEE-iz-um): Refers to a group of religions that are based on belief in one God. They are based on the belief that God is real and that He created the world. Theism says that God is active in the world, and there are no other gods beside Him.

Theistic (thee-IS-tik): An adjective used to describe a belief in one God.

Transcendence (tran-SEN-duns): The greatness of God in relation to His creation. He is above the world in every respect of power and glory.

Tribulation (TRIB-yew-LAY-shun): Severe oppression, affliction, suffering, or trouble of any kind. The New Testament refers to a time of "great tribulation," which is a time of trouble that will cover the world near the end of time. Or it may simply predict the awful sufferings people experienced when Jerusalem was destroyed in A.D. 70. Christians understand this in different ways, depending on their views of eschatology.

Wesleyan (WES-lee-un): An adjective that describes a person, doctrine, or denomination that holds to the teachings of John Wesley, especially his teaching about entire sanctification. This is the way this word is used most often in this book. The word also describes a member of The Wesleyan Church.

Zionism (ZIE-un-iz-um): An international movement in the 20th century for the establishment of a Jewish national community in Palestine and later for the support of modern Israel.